Early Bird Special!!!

And 174 Other Signs that You Have Become a Senior Citizen

TV Jose a great Kiwanian and friend.

By

Senior Citizens Mike and Jeanne Piedmonte

Mike and Jeanne

This book is a work of fiction. Places, events, and situations in this story are purely fictional. Any resemblance to actual persons, living or dead, is coincidental.

ISBN: 1-4107-0537-4 (e-book)
ISBN: 1-4107-0538-2 (Paperback)

This book is printed on acid free paper.

1stBooks - rev. 01/27/03

Acknowledgements

Our thanks go to Lucy and Mike Realo and to Joan and Dick Huber for their valuable input. And we especially thank our editor, Aimee Piedmonte.

And thanks, too, to all the Senior Citizens with whom we have shared tales about the joys and woes of this interesting passage through life.

Some of these essays first appeared in the San Francisco Examiner (San Francisco CA); The Morning Call (Allentown PA); the Sun News (Myrtle Beach SC) and Active Times Magazine.

Contents

Tell-Tale "Health" Signs

You have a good ear and a bad ear

You can dial your doctor's number without looking it up

You have your own decorated pillbox

You log more miles at night going to and from the bathroom than you do on your daily walk

You know more about your prescription medicines than your pharmacist does

You can't get into or out of your car without grunting

You show up a half-hour early for your doctor appointments "in case they can take me in early"

You need a sweater on your shoulders 340 days a year to "keep the chill off"

You wear a jogging outfit for any occasion except jogging

You experience all the side effects listed on any prescription or over-the-counter drug

You know where the rest rooms are in every store in which you shop

You are on a first-name basis with your doctor's entire office staff

You've developed your own system for remembering which pills to take and when to take them

You are not talking about vehicle fuel when the subject turns to gas

You recognize all the symptoms in prostrate, bladder, and constipation advertisements

You cannot understand how two cups of coffee can turn into four quarts of urine

Your mind wakes you up way before your body gets you up

You find yourself more outgoing and patient, mostly because of spending so much time as an Out-Patient.

You've been going to your gynecologist for so long that she recognizes your face

You know that Guy Lombardo is not a male physical ailment

You know that triglycerides are not used to make homemade bombs

You have become philosophical about physical ailments and say such things as, "There are lots of people who have it worse than me" or "I'm just glad to be able to get out of bed in the morning"

Mike and Jeanne Piedmonte

Hear, Hear!!

When I was age 20, I could hear a demure voice two rooms away. At age 35, I could hear the deep breathing of my children two floors above. At age 50, I could hear the drip of a faucet two floors below. But, alas, now that I'm a Senior Citizen I have one good ear and one bad ear. And I don't hear diddlysquat.

Having only one ear that can hear higher frequencies and that can clearly distinguish between words has advantages as well as disadvantages. Here are just a few: Since I usually cannot hear the preacher's sermon I assume God didn't intend it to apply to me anyway. My wife's anger is easily measured by its increasingly higher frequency, which even my good ear cuts out on after a certain level. I miss most of the conversation at parties, which I have found to be a great way to maintain friendships.

I almost never hear criticism. Screeching cats, squealing tires, and screaming babies don't bother me at all. Neither do sirens in the night, sharp tongues, or the sloppy diction of teenagers. Do I hear the shrill ring of the telephone? Forget it. Or the incessant clicking of the car's turn signal miles after the turn has been made? Never happen. Can I hear the swishing sound of a silk nightie on silk bed sheets? Only in my dreams.

Often not being able to distinguish between words has its embarrassing moments. Once I thanked someone for the compliment, "Your beard is really great!" only to find out what had been said was "Your beard is really gray!" Of course, having only one good ear also has its funny moments, as when I thought the announced church hymn was, "Wise up, Jerusalem."

So if hearing has become a problem, get a hearing aid, you say. Or stand closer to the speaker, learn to lip read, or turn up the volume. Sure, easy for you to say, but I don't know of anyone who enjoys having a mechanical device stuck in his or her ear. And what are you supposed to do with your pinkie finger if you don't have an empty ear to stick it into? Besides, hearing aids don't work for everybody. And, okay, there's the vanity factor. It's hard to look cool when wearing a hearing aid.

Regarding the suggestion to stand closer to the speaker or learn to read lips, please! We are all in the faces of each other enough as it is. Besides, if you need to get that close to hear someone, you probably are already wearing bifocals. It's neck-breakingly hard enough looking at a computer screen. I would hate to imagine what focusing in on a pair of moving lips would entail.

As to turning up the volume: Does the world really need louder talk radio stations, louder television automobile commercials, and louder movie bomb explosions?

So I have to face up to it. I'm a Senior Citizen with a good ear and a bad one. And the truth be known, I don't hear that well out of either of them.

But sometimes in those occasional brief moments of introspection, I catch myself wondering whether I don't hear as well as I used to. Or whether it's that I don't listen as much.

Everything a Senior Male Needs to Know About Seeing a Doctor for a Prostate Exam

We senior males get to see physicians more often than the younger male population.

Lucky us.

A trip to the doctor doesn't have to be traumatic or frustrating if a senior male is prepared to deal with the doctor and the staff on equal terms. However, since your chance of achieving this is about as small as a needle prick, here are some tips to help senior males get through their appointment with the doctor:

Making the appointment

Always schedule an appointment for the afternoon. Mid afternoon is best since that will give the doctor and the staff a chance to have their lunches and hopefully be in a better mood. You don't want a grouchy nurse giving you a shot or an irritated doctor giving you a prostate exam.

Making afternoon appointments does have one disadvantage: The doctor and the staff are ALWAYS running an hour or so late. So the naïve senior who shows up a half-hour early "in case they can take me in early" will now have an hour and a half wait. Some good advice is to call the office and ask how late the doctor is running and then time your appearance accordingly. Unfortunately, many senior males do not like to make such a call. Or they just don't have any place better to be. Either way, remember that you are off to a good start if you plan your appointment wisely.

The Outer Waiting Room

Be sure to bring your own entertainment, be it a book, magazine, crossword puzzle, or nail clippers. It is best not to speak to your fellow senior patients-in-waiting. However, if so inclined to make conversation be sure you do NOT ask, "How are you today?"

I suspect that one of the reasons for the long wait in the Outer Office is to bore the senior patient-in-waiting into a near comatose state. This condition is helpful to the doctor and staff when it comes to taking your blood pressure and not having to speak to you in terms that you might otherwise have some interest in understanding.

The Inner Waiting Room (Nurse pre-check and doctor exam room)

Always be nice and friendly with the nurses. They are the ones who not only will weigh you and give you injections, but they are the ones who will answer your questions about prescriptions, insurance, and sometimes even explain what is wrong with you in layman's English.

After the nurse is finished with your vital signs, you are left to wait for the doctor in the exam room. I suspect that this room was designed to see if you suffer from claustrophobia. And just in case you don't, the walls of the room are crowded with graphic drawings and charts showing all your vital organs and several of your not-so-vital ones. Any of these drawings and charts is capable of inducing a sickness of its own. So it is best to stick to your own entertaining material. Be aware of the temperature in the exam room. You are probably being secretly tested for signs of hypothermia and susceptibility to frostbite.

If you have ever considered meditating, this is a good time and place to start. Blanking your mind will help while away the eternity before the doctor slips on that latex glove.

When it comes to the exam by the doctor, use a "don't ask, don't tell" philosophy. All your symptoms should be on a need-to-know basis. Remember, as soon as you tell a doctor a symptom you will be whisked off to a specialist so that you can become someone else's medical—and legal—problem.

Even with all these good tips to guide you, a senior male is still much better off seeing his doctor, not by appointment at the office, but by chance at some social affair or sporting event. That way you can give the good doctor the finger instead of the other way around.

Where Has All the 'Good Stuff' Gone?

As a Senior Citizen, one of the things I miss most is being able to eat anything that I want to, when I want to, and in whatever quantities my heart desires.

Heart. Now there's the rub.

Everybody has his or her own definition of "the good old days." Mine is when I was able to eat greasy, fatty, oily, starchy, salty, and sugary stuff.

Back then, I flipped over marbled steak with French fries, inch-thick undercooked burgers with French fries, chip steak sandwiches with French fries. Heck, ketchup-drowned French fries with French fries! I relished all-pork hot dogs with sauerkraut and sour pickles.

I lusted after lard-crusted fruit pies that had been put on windowsills to cool. I carried candy bars for snacks.

Four of my closest friends, Pastrami, Salami, Pepperoni, and Bologna accompanied me to swimming holes and on hikes.

Butter and bacon, sausage and shrimp, cookies and chocolate, caramels and creams, cheese and cannolis, alfredo sauces, whole milk, and regular soda were among the staples of my diet. Diet? I'll have to check an old dictionary; I don't think that word even existed before 1990.

Now most of the food and drink that pass through my alcohol-parched lips is un-, de-, -free, non-, reduced, skim, low-, lite, and generally tasteless.

As a Senior Citizen, I also miss not being able to eat when I want to. No longer do I seem able to indulge in donuts after dances, midnight raids on the refrigerator, snacks of cold leftovers, sweets between meals, wine with lunch, and sandwiches right before bedtime Or, late-night pizza after studying, beers before, during, and after ball games, malts after movies, and ice cream anytime.

Now about the only things I can chew on whenever I want are antacid, anti-gas, and anti-diarrhea products.

Finally, as a senior, I miss not eating as much as I used to. In high school, a four-sandwich lunch barely sufficed. Second and third helpings of everything from pasta to pork chops were common. When it came to desserts, gluttony was not a sin but a blessing to look forward to.

Now, darn it, I avoid all-you-can-eat buffets. My digestive system can't handle them so I don't feel I get my money's worth. Chinese restaurants are not as much fun as they used to be. I now ask for doggie bags in family restaurants. And worst of all, I now quit after only one piece of pie.

However, I often remind myself that a lot of the food that we seniors indulged in and enjoyed in our younger days is now considered bad for your heart.

Perhaps that's why down deep in this particular senior's heart, I'm glad that I ate all that good greasy, fatty, oily, starchy, and sugary stuff when it was just that—"good."

'Push Our Luck' and Other Senior Exercises

Now, of course, many of us senior women heed the abundance of advice from the health professionals and other well-meaning individuals, organizations, and various government agencies. We walk or jog. We play tennis or golf. We swim. We stretch. We garden. We use treadmills and free weights.

You would think that this would be the end of all these efforts and admonishments to encourage us not to slack off in any way. If we don't do more and more exercising, we're told that our old bones will disintegrate faster than a dysfunctional family at the funeral of a rich relative.

Frankly, I'm sick of it. Off our sore backs, you youngn's! What you don't know is that nature provides us senior women with plenty of exercise in the course of any particular day, even if we never took a word of your advice.

Let's start with this insistence that we walk more. We senior women get plenty of this type exercise just walking the long halls in hospitals to visit relatives and friends, not to mention the "walking the hall" routine when we are recuperating from operations ourselves. Throw in a couple of walks with the dog each day, a couple of shopping trips to the supermarkets and malls each week and you'll see that we really don't have to go to any forced marches on hiking trails.

About this latest craze, weight lifting, let me say that we senior women get plenty of weight lifting exercise pressing ourselves out of bed each morning, pushing ourselves out of chairs, pulling our husbands away from television sets, and lifting our grandchildren. And our morning constitutional provides many of us with all the stomach-crunching exercise we need for strong abs.

Opening child-proof containers provides us with plenty of isometric type exercise. Many nights I hurt more from trying to open an aspirin bottle that I do from the arthritis pain. Jar lids these days all require an abundant supply of scalding water and heavy duty thumping on countertops before they can finally be forced open. And I could starve to death in the time it takes me to open a bag of pretzels or potato chips.

Steps are no longer something that we can leap in a single bound. Or, for that matter, even take two at a time. Now there are days when each darn step requires the determination of giving birth.

As for stretching exercises, just watch a senior woman trying to put on a pair of socks or pantyhose, lace her shoes, or hook her bra. Then tell us we need to spend more time stretching.

Oh, there are lots of other natural exercises we get without any effort on our parts: We spend a lot of time "rolling our eyes" at what we see going on all around us. We spend hours just trying to "look the other way." We zipper our lips and grit our teeth at the way our kids are raising our grandkids. We are all on the pro wrestling circuit when it comes to "grappling with life." And each morning when we get up, we know darn well we are once again about to "push our luck."

Tell-Tale "Family" Signs

You've wished you could have skipped having children and gone straight to having grandchildren

Your children are old enough to throw a wedding anniversary party for the two of you

You suspect that when the kids say, "where there's a will there's a way," they are talking about their inheritances

You take your grandchildren to a playground and the young mothers indulge you with a smile

You tell people that your children never gave you any problems

You are taking a computer course so you know what the heck your grandchildren are talking about

Your children have started to tell you how you should live your life

Your grandkids tell you that your house "smells funny"

Your family once had a "victory garden" and depended on it for food

Your sentences often begin with, "When I was your age..."

Your children tell you that the methods you used to raise them will not work today

You don't relish the thought of week-long visits from your children and grandchildren

The 25-year old baby furniture that you saved in the attic simply will not do by today's safety standards

You call your children for help with household projects

Your children now invite you to their homes for the holidays

You are *expected* to be available for baby sitting as needed.

Seven Do's and Do not's for Modern Day Grandparenting

Probably the worst kept secret in Senior Citizen Land is that having grandchildren is a lot more fun than was having children.

But being a grandparent isn't as easy as it used to be. We've talked to many other seniors and the consensus is that most of us barely knew our grandparents. Grandparenting then wasn't something that was *done*, except maybe for an occasional pat on the head or a terse command to do (or more likely, not to do) something or told to "be good" or to "be quiet." (For you young readers, there used to be an expression, "children should be seen but not heard." Imagine that.) Yes, back then, strong matriarchal and patriarchal barriers existed that were not crossed, and especially not by mere youngsters.

Today, grandparenting is different primarily because we are more *involved* with our grandkids. We have lowered the barriers so that they now climb over them and sometimes all over us.

As a result of the familial familiarity, many seniors are confused about their roles as grandparents so here are seven do's and don'ts for modern-day grandparenting that you won't find in any textbook:

1. When "sitting" with your grandkids, be sure to give them lots of sugar right before their parents are to pick them up. Goodies will vary depending on their ages, but candy is always good and easy to dispense. Sugar binges will make you very popular with the

grandkids while at the same time discouraging your children from asking you to sit too often.

2. Do instill some sense of ethnic heritage into your grandchildren, particularly the language of your immigrant parents or grandparents. The best way to accomplish this is to inject a couple of naughty words into your teaching. Any words that are followed by a giggle will be remembered.

3. Do instill some sense of history into your grandchildren. Do not depend on history books or courses to do this. They do not provide the personal touch that only grandparents can provide. For example, World War II stories about food and gas rationing. And, of course, don't forget the "walking miles in the snow to get to school" stories.

4. Do not tell your teenage grandchildren anything that they do not want to hear. That is the job of your children, their parents. Don't deprive your children of having to tell their kids that he can't get a tattoo on his arm or she a ring in her navel. (This is also a great way to get even with your children for once having been teens themselves.)

5. Do not watch your grandchildren perform unless they are very good at what they do. Whether it is a soccer match, baseball game, dance recital, or band concert, avoid these activities unless your grandchild is a natural athlete or a minor prodigy of some sort. Your grandkids will love you all the more for not being there when they take a called third strike, or miss an entire page of music.

6. Do take your grandchildren to restaurants if you can do so without having their parents come along.

Mike and Jeanne Piedmonte

Nothing ruins a good lunch more than well-meaning but meddlesome manner-minded parents.

7. Buy your grandchildren gifts, but do not ever give them cash. They will spend it even faster than your children do.

If there is a bottom line to modern-day grandparenting, it is this: You do not want your grandchildren behaving as if they were your children. That would spoil all the fun.

Nonna, Where Have You Gone?

The morning after our first grandchild was born I was totally delighted. The second morning I wasn't quite as elated. Sometime during the early hours of that second day I had looked over at my wife of 31 years and it dawned on me that I was now married to a grandmother. (In Italian, a nonna.)

How can this be, I wondered. This woman beside me cannot possibly be a grandmother. She is nothing like either of my grandmothers, or her Irish ones either, for that matter. Was I looking at grandmothers from a different perspective? Or are the grandmothers of today so different from those of my childhood?

Looking back, my grandmothers:

Sat in rocking chairs
Knitted scarves and hats
Crocheted doilies and tablecloths
Spent a lot of time over hot stoves (coal burning ones at that) busy making soups, roasts and "gravies."
Shelled peas and beans
Waited for their kids and families to come visit
Ate "killer" foods loaded with lard and sugar
Never heard of the expression, "nutrition pyramid"
Never ate in restaurants
Said their rosaries faithfully
Never traveled in anything larger than an automobile
Wore housedresses and aprons all day long
Wore sturdy shoes with chunky heels

Had a wooden spoon or a "mopino" (dishtowel) in their hands
Dampened and starched clothes before ironing
Hung all clothes on a wash line to dry regardless of the season
Had gray hair
Wore their hair in tight buns
Obeyed my grandfathers
Knew how to sew clothes
Knew how to mend socks and holes in pockets
Knew how to "make do"
Waited on us with treats of homemade bread and homemade jams
Got their exercise by using washboards and rug beaters
Preferred produce peddlers and farmers markets to the A&P stores
Never wore anything but black after the grandfathers died

Are grandmothers of today different from those of our youth? Of course. But their grandchildren don't know or care about these differences.

As far as the grandkids know their grandmothers are supposed to:

Work outside the home
Instruct them to help themselves to the treats in the freezer
Wear jeans and jogging suits
Join book clubs
Dye their hair
Hop on planes
Pop in on their families

Run on treadmills
Send cash on holidays, birthdays, and graduations
Visit fast food places with them
Make restaurant reservations, and
Take golf, tennis, scuba diving and Yoga lessons

But we guys who are married to these modern-day nonnas know the difference. Especially that one about *obeying* our grandfathers.

How to Cope with Married Children

The famous lawyer, Clarence Darrow, once said "The first half of our lives is ruined by our parents, and the second half by our children." By now, for most of us Senior Citizens your "issue" (as the lawyers call them) are not merely *child* children, but now *adult* children—at least to hear them tell it. So here we'll examine some important areas in which we must learn to cope with our offspring as they age.

Most of the time, thank God, adult children leave the nest. But sometimes they come back, hopefully bringing grandchildren with them and staying a week or less, preferably less. Unfortunately, however, more frequently our children are divorcing (about 50% at last count) and coming back to the nest for more than a week, sometimes way more than a week. So in surviving adult children, we'll first examine how to cope with these short-term and long-term visits.

Short-Term Visits

Depending on the ages of your grandchildren, short term visits usually begin with the kids leaping from the car, anxious to embrace you and tell you all about the latest whatever—pet (guess where Meggie peed!), school (we got new computers!), social activities (our soccer coach quit 'cause all the parents hate him). As the grandkids become teens, they are less likely to want to share any information or emotions with anyone so ancient and so out of touch with what life is all about. (Though sharing your money with them is still cool.) So try not to pat your teenage grandchildren on their heads as this will only further reinforce their feelings that you think they are still babies (which, of course, they still are and always will be).

Regardless of the size of the kitchen, short-term visits usually mean unaccustomed kitchen clutter. With an additional two adults (one of them being your son who still thinks there are popsicles in the refrigerator), mealtimes and snack times can get crowded. If the visiting adult child is a son, keep him out of the kitchen! He will only open wrapped cold cuts, leave plastic containers partially sealed, drink from milk and juice cartons, and give you cooking hints.

Regardless of their ages, always have grandchildren eat at different times from their parents. This way such mealtime unpleasantness as scolding, swilling, and spilling will not spoil your meals. Also, since they are at your house for such a short period, let everybody eat what they want and how much or little of it, too. Fact is, to really survive kitchen warfare your best bet is to head for the nearest diner while your company eats at home. And make sure you don't call first before returning home. They will want you to bring some take-out.

Long-Term Visits

Adult children coming home on a long-term basis as a result of some circumstance as divorce, unavailability of employment, or inability to graduate from a higher-learning institution all present a unique problem—how do you do away with them without their bodies being found. Seriously though, this might be a good time to more fully explore the idea of purchasing a condo that you've been kicking around the past couple of years. You know, that nice community development in Florida, or the one in the Southwest—whichever is farther away. One last thought: remember it was your spouse that you promised to stick with, not your adult kids.

Visiting the Homes of Your Adult Children

Visiting (and therefore coping) with your adult children at their homes is always a challenge. Perhaps the primary survival rule here is not to expect their places to be as neat, clean, organized, or landscaped as well as yours is. Clothes from the laundry or for the laundry, under-bed dustballs, stacked sinks and littered yards are the trademarks of the harried two-income families of today. Therefore, ignore the unmade beds, the piles of clothes on the dressers, the uncapped toothpaste tubes, the pieces of toys on the floor (never, *ever*, walk barefoot in any home where there are grandchildren!) Fact is, ignore the sincere urging of your adult children to stay at their home. Instead, opt for a nice nearby quiet motel where the bed is made, there aren't any fingerprints on the TV screen, and the bathroom doesn't have to be locked when you are using it.

The Raising of Your Grandchildren

Now this is a touchy subject, but some things need to be said. Here is a fact, not an opinion: *Your adult children are not raising their children as well as they should be.* There, now it's out in the open. Show this accusation to your adult children (better yet, buy them their own copy of this book so they can read it over and over).

Lovable as they are, your grandkids can be spoiled, brazen, outspoken, ungrateful, and oftentimes disrespectful—and these are when they are not tired or hungry. Then sometimes it gets ugly. This, of course, is the fault of their parents who are much too anxious to spend "quality time" with their children in as pleasant an atmosphere as possible.

To cope with the lousy job of child rearing being done by our offspring, we have to put a couple of things in context. For one, we did not have "quality" time with our kids. What we had was *time* for them. And even if we didn't, there was no guilt associated with it. As long as the kids understood their place in the family—and that they would be whacked if they forgot—things would work out.

So how to cope with the behavioral breakdowns of your grandchildren? You keep your lips zipped, or to put it more bluntly, YOU MIND YOUR OWN BUSINESS. Chances are that you won't be around to see how the grandkids turn out anyway. Meanwhile, there's nothing more delightful than a grandchild who's been "bad" all day who, before going to bed, hugs and kisses you while cuddled up with you on the sofa.

Sons-and Daughters-In Law

A couple of words about sons-in law and daughters-in-law are in order if your relationships with them are not going well. Keep in mind that as the fathers or mothers of your grandchildren, they don't have to get along with you to the extent that you have to get along with them. *You* are the one who wants to bring everyone into the fold of your family.

Actually, getting along well with young in-laws is quite simple if you just keep in mind that no matter whom your children married, you probably would never have been totally satisfied with their choice of mates. Let's face it, nobody is good enough for your offspring. This is true even if your kids were voted "Least Likely to Succeed" by their classmates at the juvenile detention center where they got their GEDs.

Money Matters (you damn well bet it does!!)

Inheritances, loans, and gifts to adult children can present major sibling squabbling if not handled wisely. With inheritances you don't really need worry about their conflicts or jealousies, so feel free and clear to divvy up your bucks as you deem appropriate. Whatever their reactions, they will be of no concern to you.

Loans and outright gifts are another matter—you're going to have to live with generosity which favors one or the other. If you have thought about this possible predicament early enough and only had had one child, you could have saved yourself some stress when one or the other comes calling with need of ready cash. Treat each loan as a bank would and have a clear and manageable repayment understanding. Otherwise, call it a gift and remember that a gift given to one should be given to each or there will be hell to pay. You can bank on that.

We know what you are thinking now. It's your money and you will darn well do with it what you want to and when you want to. But when you think about it, that's not true. The only money in that estate of yours that is truly yours—is that which you have already spent.

Where 'Snowbirds' Come From

Two childhood rites of passage occur when you discover that there is no Santa Claus who brings gifts, nor a stork who delivers babies. But, in truth, these discoveries were not all that startling. You had had your suspicions about these tales for some time.

We find ourselves in the same situation when we are much older. We suspect that we are no longer middle-aged, but we have to hear it from the likes of AARP, and later the Social Security Office, and then the good folks from Medicare.

But they are "outsiders" and not the personal insights of someone close. No, in this case it's your children and grandchildren who let you know when you have made the passage to "senior." And usually, they will let you know in not so subtle ways. Here are just some of them:

Your children inform you that they are throwing you a wedding anniversary party and that *they* are paying for it.

Your children start taking turns having the families over for the holidays.

They insist on driving when they go anywhere with you, even if it's in your car.

Your children tell you they never gave you any problems as teen-agers, as if you can't remember that far back.

They instinctively take you by the arm when going down stairs.

Your children indicate an interest in whether you have an updated will and where it is kept.

Your children buy you a Super AAA membership *and* a cell phone for your vacation trips.

They question whether it is "wise" for you to do something or to go someplace.

Your children call you often to see how you are doing.

Your children ask you for the name and phone number of your doctor.

They show an interest in your medications.

Your children want to go inside the exam room with you to be sure you know what the doctor is telling you.

Your grandchildren think it's funny when they have to shout when speaking to you on the telephone.

Your grandchildren like to feel your skin and touch your veins.

Your grandkids ask if those are really your teeth.

Your grandkids think anything you can do on a computer is really "cool."

Your grandkids ask, "Can you still have fun when you are old?"

Your grandkids think you should have a pet because you might get lonely.

Now don't get me wrong. I know we seniors appreciate the fact that our children and grandchildren help ease us into our latter years. But just as a kid wants to ignore the facts of life and cling to the myths, so do we want to escape the truth.

This is why so many of us become "snowbirds" and fly away for the winter. We then can walk in the sun and the sand and pick seashells, and be kids again ourselves even if for only a short while.

(This article first appeared in Active Times Magazine)

Grandfathers Don't Have to Take Any Crap

As a grandfather, you quickly learn that you have a lot more freedom than you did as a father of a newborn child or toddler. Now you don't have to get involved in those activities that kept you occupied during the pregnancy months and the first couple of years of the baby's life. For example, grandfathers do not have to:

attend baby showers
feel the baby kicking in the womb
go shopping for maternity clothes
listen to horror stories about swollen feet, backaches, and stretch marks
be in the delivery room during the birth
look at severed umbilical cords
look at circumcised penises
bathe squirmy infants
feel the soft spot in the baby's head
hold infants who have crapped in their diapers
change "messy" diapers
feed warm bottles of smelly formula to infants
be vomited on
be burped on
console screaming infants with contorted faces
squirt sticky liquids on your wrists to test for bottle temperatures.
cotton swab infant's ears and nose
feed baby in the middle of the night

Mike and Jeanne Piedmonte

console a spouse who has to feed the baby in the middle of the night
call a pediatrician's office in the middle of the night
comfort a spouse who has to call a pediatrician's office in the middle of the night
give a feverish baby a cool bath in the middle of the night
take a baby's anal temperature
feed infants who are squirming and trying to get out of a high chair
feed any child who has a spoon or other potentially lethal weapon in his/her hand
crawl on hand and knees and peek around corners
give the baby medicine
examine stool colors
speak baby talk and otherwise sound like an idiot when talking to a baby
console teething babies
go rushing out of church with screaming baby
catch baby's every move on film or video
remember all the "cute" things baby has said.

But what's really nice about being a grandfather is that you can do any or all of the above—if you want to!

The Rules That Govern Babies

Becoming a father is a highly emotional experience. It is one that does not lend itself to any kind of objective analysis of what babies do during those first 24 to 48 hours after birth.

Now that I'm a grandfather, I can take a more detached, third-party view of newborns. What amazes me most about them is that they apparently are born into this world governed by certain rules that they must abide by. How newborns know these rules, I do not know. But that such rules do exist, I do know.

Rule one is that all newborns must look alike. None can be cuter or more handsome than the others. Their eyes must be mere slits, their hair (if any) wild, their skin blotchy, and their fists clenched, as if ready to defend themselves.

I'm convinced that hospitals all have the same generic photo of some newborn that was taken many years ago, and this is the photo that they distribute to all parting moms and proud dads.

The next rule is that newborns must pretend not to be too smart. They must feign a level of intelligence below that of their parents. It is not until these newborns reach their teens that they will expose the superior intellect that they have hidden all those years.

A third rule that seems to be inherently obeyed by newborns is that they must be gluttons. They must not simply need food on a regular basis, they must also demand it. And they must not just want a generous quantity of milk, they must want to be able to devour nipple and breast or bottle too, if given the opportunity.

Another rule is that newborns must pretend that they are uncoordinated and unable to help themselves in any way. Any letting on that they could fend for themselves if they wanted to would only make their parents feel unnecessary and unwanted. These stressful emotions newborns will bestow on their parents in fifteen or sixteen years, but for now they must be content to stare blankly and thrash wildly about between naps and feedings.

The next rule is that newborns must cry a lot. This is a cardinal rule. And not just when they are hungry or wet, though these alone would provide hours of excuse to cry, scream, hold their breath, and in general intimidate and terrorize their parents. Parents' emotional states at this point in their lives is one step below panic (if it's their first child) or despair (if it's not their first).

The final rule apparently is that newborn children must never fit into their clothes the way their parents would like them to. Their feet must never be completely into the little foot pockets of pajamas, or their hats smartly on their heads, or their diapers snugly against their bottoms. Evidently, disarray and disorder are a must for newborns.

However, as we all know there are exceptions to every rule. This is true, too, of the rules governing newborn children. Take our latest granddaughter, Gracie, for example. She is by far the cutest kid in the hospital nursery. Even the nurses say they had never seen so pretty a baby. Or one so good natured. And is she ever smart! Let me tell you what she did yesterday...

TELL-TALE
"CHRONOLOGICAL" SIGNS

Your baseball cap has the name of a World War II ship on it

You once had a two-party telephone line

You've had your retirement watch so long that it now needs the battery replaced

You know that Depression was an era, not a state of mind

Your dentist has stopped sending you "check up" reminders

Your first house cost less than half of what your last car did

You can't bring yourself to call some young priest, "Father"

Your children wore cloth diapers

You are asked questions by a family member who is interested in genealogy

You recognize the "big band" sound when you hear it and you can remember the words to all those love ballads

You know what "mairzy doats" means

You realize you would be the December part of a May-December romance

Your main source of erotica when you were an adolescent was comic books, movie star magazines, and novels like "Forever Amber"

You know that "spooning" was not something done with utensils

You were a USO hostess

You know who "Da Schnoz" was

Your birth year doesn't appear on the astrology placemats in Chinese restaurants

You've used coal ashes on icy sidewalks when you were a kid

Your tattoos have become illegible

You've swooned over "ole blue eyes"

You know that a soda jerk usually wasn't a jerk at all and he did a lot more than squirt soda

You watched the "$64,000 Question"

You can finish the term, Horn & Hardart _____

You sometimes refer to a refrigerator as an "ice box"

You refer to retiring as "getting out," as in "I've been out for eight years already"

You used to mail letters instead of clicking them

You bought your ice cream from the "Good Humor Man"

You used to think a 50th high school reunion was for *really* old people.

Everyone But One at 50th Reunion Was Old

One of the great things about lasting long enough to become a Senior Citizen is that you can get to go to your 50th high school reunion.

Never mind that you never imagined that you would ever go to such an old fogie affair. You find yourself at the registration desk all decked out in a suit and wearing a tie for the first time in years, or in a new dressy dark two-piece dress you weren't too sure you would fit into. You check your name tag to make sure you are properly identified and to remind yourself whether you pre-ordered the prime rib or the stuffed flounder.

You hold on to your spouse and head for the festively decorated ballroom, knowing full well that this is a once-in-a-lifetime event. You look forward to seeing many of your classmates who also have not "passed on."

So, with great expectations, off I went with my wife to my big 5-0 reunion. And except for one lingering question that still has me somewhat upset, I had a really great time.

This was the first reunion that I had attended, and I hadn't seen many of my classmates for five decades. It turns out that this is a *really* long time. I soon realized that many of my classmates— male in particular—had aged so much!

A couple of them seemed much shorter than I remembered them. It was as if they literally had shrunk. Where once they had stood tall and confident in their athletic uniforms, they now seemed smaller than life-size. I realized that I was standing a bit round-shouldered myself, embarrassed as I was I at their misfortune.

Many of the men had hearing aids buried in their skulls. Even then I found myself speaking louder than I would have liked because they kept cupping their ears as if to protect our conversations from the background sounds of the band, which usually wasn't playing anyway. I felt so sorry for my classmates that I, too, cupped my hand to the back of one ear so as not to make them feel uncomfortable.

I couldn't get over the hair loss of the guys. Many of them had varying degrees of baldness. I was so taken aback with all the deforested domes around me that I found myself discreetly moving my hairs around to make it look as if I, too, were thinning at a faster rate than I actually am. I couldn't help noting for myself how accurate my barber is about one of his observations. He says that it seems that the balder an older guy gets the more hair grows out of his ears. He's mentioned this a couple of times while giving me a trim.

During the World War II years, when our class was just in our junior high school days, there was a war slogan about the dangers of "loose lips." The slogan for our 50th reunion could have warned about the dangers of "loose skin." I haven't seen as many wrinkles in a just-washed bed sheet! I tried to make light of all the sagging around me by joking, "Hey, we still have it. It's just that it's all a lot lower now." Everyone thought that was hilarious.

And I couldn't believe how heavy some of my old classmates have gotten. Now I admit to having put on a couple of pounds myself, but many of my classmates have really let themselves go. I thought to myself that if we put our class into our old football stadium, we'd practically have a capacity crowd. Funny, I remember thinking that as one of my classmates took the last dinner roll, which I had wanted.

The band, I was told, was contracted to play until 11:30, but I noted that when we left at 10:30 many of the other couples were already gone. They just couldn't take the nightlife any more, I guess.

So you might think that it was all the deteriorating effects of gravity and time on my poor classmates that bothered me as I moved in conversation from one to another, but that wasn't it at all.

No, what bothered and somewhat upset me was that every time I got into a conversation with different classmates, I just *know* I saw smug looks on their faces (smirks on a few of them!). Even now when I think back and reflect on that reunion, I can't imagine what they were looking so smug about when seeing me for the first time in fifty years.

Mike and Jeanne Piedmonte

I Don't Give No Respect

Much has been written and said about the demise of respect given to Senior Citizens. And it's true, we don't get the respect we deserve, except at election times.

No longer does merely being older establish you as a wise old soul and automatically worthy of respect. No longer do children sit on front porch steps while the senior member of the family pontificates from the rocking chair or swing.

Grandchildren are even worse when it comes to respecting a senior's knowledge and experience. To them everything we know is B.C.—Before Computers. After all, to many of us a "hard drive" is a well hit ball right up the middle, a mouse is something we used to catch in traps, and a keyboard is something you used to make music.

What we learned from the Depression is not applicable today. "It was a different world then," they say. What we gave for World War II is not comprehensible ("it was a different world then"). What we know of our ethnic roots is unimportant ("it was a different world then").

We are ignored by teenage clerks at grocery counters. Young bank tellers call us by our first names. And punk comics think we are funny. About the only time we hear a "Sir" or "Ma'am" is when some Generation X, Y, or Z is annoyed with us for not moving along fast enough, not understanding quickly enough, or not healing soon enough.

I used to lament this loss of respect until recently when I realized that I'm also caught up in this downward social spiral. Simply put, I don't *give* no respect (to paraphrase Rodney Dangerfield).

I think the problem is that a title no longer automatically demands my respect. For example, I don't respect lawyers anymore. Not since the Simpson murder trial have I been able to pass up telling a "lawyer joke." Doctors I'm wary about. Fear of lawsuits seems to be at the heart of too many of their referrals. The clergy seem more interested in real estate than they do religious matters.

Honest politicians? Unbiased journalists? Scrupulous corporations? Untainted unions? Reliable leaders of foreign nations? Altruistic sports team owners, managers, or players? Accountable federal law enforcement agencies? Please!!

Now, do understand that I'm generalizing. Of course there are individuals in all these categories who have gained or retained the respect due them. But unfortunately they seem to me to be the exceptions rather than the rule.

And I admit that it's not all simply cynicism on my part. Some of it is my age, too. For the life of me, I can't call a 25-year old Catholic priest "Father." Or a 30-year old, "Doctor." Or a 40-year old, "Boss."

Okay, do as my wife does and call me a cranky old man. But better yet, call me by that one title that damn well still better automatically demand respect. Address me as Curmudgeon.

Everything Senior Women Need To Know About Computers

As a grandmother, I have to admit that I am pleased with myself for trying to learn about computers. Not that I have done this willingly, not that I haven't procrastinated, not that I haven't shed a tear or two in frustration, and not that I have bridged the gap between software and sanity.

But I have accepted the futility of resistance. For example, in any given beginners computer class, the instructor will ask the Senior Citizens why they want to learn about computers. I don't know why they ask this each session because they basically get the same answers, "So I can know what my grandkids are talking about," and "So I can keep up with the times."

So to try to know what the grandkids are talking about— at least in this one area—we have had to learn about some basic computer parts, such as a CPU, keyboard, CD-ROM, mouse, modem, and motherboard. We also have had to learn about such things as Windows and, of course, THE INTERNET.

Following is this senior lady's attempt to come to terms with the terms of this modern technology—and still keep a sense of humor:

CPU stands for Can't Possibly Understand. It has to do with a little silicon chip that is now called a Pentium. CPUs also come in various speeds that are measured in megahertz and gigahertz, which are not like miles-per-hour or anything so comprehensible.

Computer keyboards are pretty much similar to typewriter keyboards, but they also have several other keys to the right of your "typewriter" keyboard. These keys say things like Home, End, Delete, Insert, Page Up, Page Down, and some are just keys with arrows on them. To the right of this bunch of keys are a bunch of numbered keys that say things like Home, End, Delete, Insert, Page Up, Page Down, and these also have arrows on them. (Frankly, for all the so-called computer efficiency you hear about, the keyboard seems terribly redundant.)

A CD-ROM is like the disk you use in a CD player only these play video pictures as well as sound. But the really neat part is that your CD-ROM plays anywhere from 50 to 70 times faster than standard time (I am not sure where daylight savings time fits into all this).

A mouse is a mouse unless, of course, it is plugged into the rear of a computer, then it's a serial mouse or a PS2 mouse. You click or double click the left side of the mouse. Do not click the right side of the mouse or the computer will blow up! Just kidding, you do occasionally right click for some things as transferring a file to a disk. In addition to clicking your mouse, you can also roll it on a special pad (I hope this doesn't sound like I'm talking dirty) and it will move a little rectangular block or arrow around on your screen. This lets you quickly be anywhere on the computer screen that you want to be, but it does not answer that old philosophical question, "Why am I here?"

The modem is an internal or external device that hooks you up to a telephone line that lets you call AOL or one of the many other on-line service providers. These companies then connect you to the Internet so that you can e-mail your friends instead of just picking up the phone and *talking* to them.

Windows is a computer operating system that has replaced lots of words with pictures so now even illiterates can compute by clicking and peeking into the pictures (windows) on the screen. I guess you have to believe that if an eight-year old can use it…

Random Access Memory (RAM) is a special part of your system memory that Windows uses. The only important thing about RAM to remember is that the more the better. At first there were just a couple of megabytes (megabytes being 1,000 times 1,000 bytes, or characters. Still with me? Then there was 16, then 32, then 64. Last I knew they were up to 128 and probably still going.

When I first heard the term, motherboard, I thought of a house-bound mother with no interests beyond "As the World Turns." But as it turns out, a motherboard is a thin flat piece of circuit board, which evidently has sockets to accept the various PC components such as the hard drive and random access memory. In other words, it's the place where everything ties together. Maybe that's where the "mother" part comes from.

The only thing you really have to know about the Internet is this: Don't do or say *anything* important on it. Your message can easily be lost in cyberspace, read by practically anyone in the world, and may well end up in a government file. As one wag has put it, when it comes to the Internet at least, if you aren't paranoid, you're crazy.

The above is, of course, meant to be a mere spattering of computereeze. Computer books for dummies alone contain thousands of pages so don't think you are ever going to actually get up to speed on these things. But that's not the important thing; what is important is that if you don't have access to newspapers, magazines, encyclopedias, movies, libraries, or live-people friends, a computer is the panacea for your predicament.

Of course, there are always some people who might say you should get a life. But what do you care, as long as it's not your grandkids saying it.

Mike and Jeanne Piedmonte

'Going Places' Has Different Meaning for Senior Citizens

When I was a young man, a night out meant that me and my sweetie would be spending the evening together. Now that I'm a Senior Citizen, a night out means that me and my teeth won't be spending the night together.

Now please understand that just because I'm a senior doesn't mean that I don't still like going places and doing things. It's just that the places and things somehow have changed. For example, when I was a young man...

I went to see old friends at parties at their homes. Now I get to see old friends mostly at viewings in funeral homes.

I went to dances early to be sure that I would make my way around the dance floor a couple of times a night. Now I go to bed early and make my way to the bathroom a couple of times a night.

I went to a lot of noisy concerts for kicks. Now I go to the ear doctor for adjustments to my hearing aid.

I drank martinis on a regular basis. Now I drink Metamucil to stay regular.

I used to go to study halls and pay attention to my p's and q's. Now I go to bingo halls and pay attention to my B's and O's

I used to go to publishers' offices and give samples of my stories. Now I go to doctors' offices and give samples of my stools.

I would flirt in nightclubs with the barmaids. Now I flirt in nursing homes with the nurses aides

I knew where the "Active Wear" department was in department stores. Now I know where the rest rooms are in every store.

I had a father to "straighten me out." Now that phrase takes on new meaning and has become the job of a chiropractor.

I used to go to the pharmacy to buy vitamins to keep my vigor up. Now I go to buy Viagra to keep my morale up.

Don't get me wrong, I don't mind going to these different places now that I'm a senior. No, what bothers me is that to get to all these new places, somewhere along the way I had to turn a corner. But I don't remember doing that.

Tell-Tale "Recall" Signs

You can recall some of the inhabitants of (Fred) Allen's Alley

You can recall when Meals on Wheels meant eating at a drive-in restaurant

You can't recall the last time you bought a necktie

You can barely remember what you did at your job

You can remember when a monitor was a person who watched you, not a machine that you watch.

You recall when a doctor also asked about the rest of your family

You can recall when a handyman showed up when he said he would

You can't recall the last time you bought a feminine hygiene product

You remember when "draft" meant more than a beer on tap

You can remember when girls got "knocked up"

You can remember when "adult" films were called stag movies

You can remember when "Coke" only had one meaning

You can recall when airplanes all had propellers

You can remember your mother using a washboard and Fels Napha soap

You recall wearing gloves as part of being "dressed up"

You recall when there were stores that sold nothing but ladies' hats

You remember the "Dragon Lady" from the Terry & the Pirates comic strip

You remember wearing a dress hat to work

You can recall buying penny candy

You can recall when children asked, "May I?..."

You remember when everyone's dog was a mutt

You recall playing kick the can, hide and seek and onesy twosy, all without adult supervision

You remember going downtown with your folks

You recall when there were worms in apples

You can remember when actors kissed with their mouths closed

Seven Tips for Overcoming Male CRS

There have been plenty of studies indicating that, unless one has a serious mental problem, aging doesn't necessarily mean a loss of memory. In other words, despite what our wives think, not all of us senior men get bad cases of CRS (Can't Remember Shit).

This is also my own personal belief. However, I have been preparing myself should I begin to lose this now vaunted memory of mine by devising the following seven tips for remembering things. Not all are surefire and all have some weaknesses. However, one or all may work if you suspect that you are coming down with a case of CRS.

1. Leave stuff about. This method precedes the making of a written or mental list. What you do is leave out on the kitchen counter, dining room table, bed, etc. the actual items you need to shop for. Example: You are running low on mouthwash. Leave the open near-empty container on the bathroom sink. Clothes to the cleaners? Leave them on the bed. Need to check the oil in your car? Well, you get the idea.

2. Memorize by association. For example, you need a haircut—think of Sophia Loren. You need to make restaurant reservations—think of Sophia Loren. Need to pick your grandchildren up at school? Think of Sophia Loren. This method doesn't always work but I still use it a lot anyway.

3. Make words from the first letters of each item you want to remember (There is a name for this method

but I can't recall what it is right now). Anyway, say you need Asparagus, Pears, Olives, X-Lax, and Yams. In this simple example, you make the word APOXY. It does get more complicated when you don't buy any vowels.

4. Don't clog up your brain with unnecessary details. Only bother memorizing those items you may forget. For example, you need butter, broccoli, and beer. Yeah, like without some concentrated effort you are going to forget the beer!

5. Go coupon and ad shopping. As much as possible, shop only for products for which you have coupons or advertisements. An ad for a car wash, a sale on tomatoes, coupons for cat litter. Taking along these little pieces of paper does wonders for not forgetting items—as long as you don't forget the little pieces of paper.

6. Use male common sense. This method assumes no wife will send her husband to the store for anything too complicated. So even if you can't remember what you are supposed to get, you know it must be something as basic as a half gallon of juice, a quart of milk, or a dozen eggs. By contrast, you know you will never have been sent to purchase laundry detergent, for instance, where you would have to know whether to buy the 44 oz., the gallon, or the 100 oz. size.

7. I know there is a seventh one, but darned if I can think of it right now. Besides, I'm in a hurry to get to the supermarket. I just remembered that we're totally out of ginko.

Why Seniors Can Never Be Rich

During a TV show that Mike and I were watching a while back, the actress Bette Midler said something like, "Once you have been poor, you can never be rich."

After some discussion, we took her remark to mean that if you can recall being poor when you were young, no matter how much wealth or estate you accumulate afterwards, it will never be enough. You will never believe that you "have enough" and that, if anything, you are at best merely "well off."

As Senior Citizens, many of us can recall being poor when we were children. In many cases, darned poor. And so we continue in many ways to do little "savings" things that show this inbred financial insecurity.

For example, go to any restaurant that offers an "early bird special," and you will find the place filled with seniors. Never mind that we regularly cook our evening meal at home hours later. On early bird special days, we are even willing to eat dinner before our grandchildren have been dismissed from school.

Senior women without food coupons in a supermarket feel absolutely naked. And if there is one thing you don't want to feel when you are a senior woman is naked. So we women roam the food aisles with our little purses bulging with coupons; the men with fists filled with scraps of paper, all searching for the manufacturers' discounts or the store's double coupons.

Seniors will go to anything that is advertised as FREE. This word is a verbal magnet to us and we will follow it anywhere—to seminars, lectures, concerts, health fairs, plays, even to injections. Anybody who believes there is no such thing as a free lunch just hasn't been hanging around a senior citizen lately. Those "lunches" are out there, and we know where they are!

Seniors travel a lot, but you won't find most of us in upscale motels and hotels along the way. These we leave with our best wishes to the business travelers on expense accounts. Instead, when we have logged our miles for the day on the interstates and tourist roads, we will select modest accommodations as long as they are clean, include a continental breakfast, and we know there won't be a dozen rigs out back with their engines running after 10 p.m.

Senior men will drive miles out of their way to get gas for pennies a gallon cheaper. So what if the gas consumed for this lowest-cost search nets us only a ten-cent savings. We don't care. It's the principle that counts.

Senior discount days at local stores fill the parking lots with elderly card-carrying women totally intent on purchasing items for their children and grandchildren, younger neighbors, and friends. Heck, we'll even shop for people we don't especially like rather than pass up that senior discount. "Wait until Wednesday. I can get it for you at 10% off" is the universal instruction given by seniors on the other six days a week.

Seniors will go to the movies at any time of the day. We would probably go to movies at 6 a.m. if we could get in at a discounted price. We already have made it profitable for the multiplexes to run matinees, the audiences mostly being refugees from senior citizen centers.

Okay, so we admit we seniors do these "savings" things. But remember, you baby boomers, X-Gen's, whatever, we seniors are the ones who came through the economic hard times of the 1930s. Most of us made it with our heads pretty much together. But we do have these idiosyncrasies when it comes to handling money. And this is because that although there are a lot of people around today who know what depression is, it's only we seniors who know what a Depression was.

Mike and Jeanne Piedmonte

Is There A Communications Problem?

I have an important question to ask you readers, but first I want to reflect on how communicating for this Senior Citizen has changed over the years.

When I was a kid in school, we wrote with a pen and ink and used blotters to avoid smears. No kidding.

Now I have a 1.0GHz processor, with 128 MB of RAM, 40 gigabytes on the hard drive, a 12X max DVDCD ROM drive, and a 17-inch monitor.

When I was a youngster, my family had a two-party line on our telephone. Yes, two families shared the same telephone line and we often had to wait before the line was clear and we could make or receive a call.

Now we have two telephone lines coming into the house so we don't have to wait until we're off the computer to make or receive a call.

When I was in high school, I used a notebook to take notes. It was one of those marbled covered books with lined pages to make sure I wrote small and straight. I took a lot of notes because even then I knew better than to trust my memory. My trusty notebook weighed in at a couple of ounces.

Now I have an electronic notebook with 128 megabytes of memory and a 20 GB hard drive, just in case. My adult notebook weighs in at a little over seven pounds, battery included.

When I was a kid, I had a pager. It went by the generic name of MOM. MOM could locate me anywhere. If she couldn't locate me directly, she had a hookup satellite system of neighborhood MOMs who could page me within minutes.

Today for my wireless messaging communications, I have a digital numeric pager that involves *real* satellite technology that allows self- and operator-dispatched messages and customized greetings.

I can remember writing letters, licking stamps, and sealing envelopes. Sometimes I walked to the nearest mailbox to deposit my letter. Other times I just left it at our mailbox for the mailman to pick up. Either way, in a couple of days my correspondent would receive the letter and quickly rip away at the envelope.

Nowadays, with the help of my 56V.90modem, I e-mail all my letters to family, friends, and even some people I have never met and probably never will. Sometimes, I simply "Compose" a new message, usually I "Reply to Author" or maybe "Reply to All." I might even "Forward" mail that I especially enjoyed. Ah, that "Send and Receive" icon. How did I ever get to be a Senior Citizen without it?

In the course of past events it sometimes became necessary to have to send a document. This involved odd-sized envelopes, odd-denomination stamps, and odd instructions for delivery.

For current events, this is no problem with my caller-ID-ready fax machine with its 99-page auto document feeder, 512k memory and 58-number auto dial and redial features.

Yes, things were different way back when I answered the phone with my hearty baritone, "Hello" instead of having my voice mail screen the call or inform one and all that I'm out or too busy doing something else to take their call.

But now back to that important question that I referred to earlier: Why is it my wife is always complaining that I don't talk to her much anymore?

Saturday Night Date, Circa 1949

The Teenage Male Prepping Process

The Teenage Female Prepping Process

Bathe in tub (very few had showers)

Bathe in tub (very few had showers)

Douse hair liberally with Vitalis or other hair slicker

Set hair in tight pin curls Wear hair in straight bangs or pageboy

Comb hair in back to create a Duck's Ass (DA) so sharp you could cut a finger on it

Don pointed bra, plain white or pastel panties, seamed nylons, garter belt, panty girdle and half or full slip.

Don boxer shorts, tee shirt, and argyl socks

Decide on dress flats, high heels, saddle shoes or penny loafers

Decide on pair of blue suede shoes, penny loafers, or dress shoes. If dress shoes, shine until they are slippery

Wear Gibson girl blouse and skirt, father or brother's dress shirt over rolled up jeans.

Wear white dress shirt with French cuffs, or plaid flannel shirt, pleated slacks with thin belt

Wear a twin sweater set, same colors, short sleeves and cardigan sweaters
Examine wristwatch,

Mike and Jeanne Piedmonte

Sport a blue or plaid sport coat with side slits, broad padded shoulders, and wide lapels

Knot a cotton knit tie with a Windsor knot that is large enough to hide your Adam's apple and half the pimples on your neck
Examine watch, religious medal, ID bracelet, rings, and tie clasp

Check wallet to see how badly deteriorated old condom is

Check wallet for money. Figure $5 should do it for a dance or movie, and drive-in restaurant afterwards

Obtain keys to stick-shift family car. Usually no problem, parents almost never go out on a Saturday night, or any other night for that matter

string of pearl necklace and matching clip-on button pearl earrings, locket on gold chain, religious necklace, class ring, birthstone ring.

Check purse for extra sanitary napkin in case "fall off the roof," or get the "monthly curse"

Check wallet for "mad money"

The Porch—Long May It Reign

When I was a youngster we had a large wooden porch on the front of our home. On those rainy days when there was no indoor Monopoly game going on or none of the usual outdoor games that goes with being boys, the porch was ideal for watching the rain.

It was deep enough so the cushioned porch glider and the old wooden high-backed rocking chair were generally secure from wetness. A large straw matting kept the rain from splattering the top of many coats of porch paint. The open railing provided no protection, really, but somehow it provided a boundary between the elements and myself.

On those days, even though in the distance lightning burned the sooty sky and thunder applauded its brother's violence, I could enjoy the quiet, the comfort, the cozy security of the blanket of rain. On those days when rain scrubbed the streets and muddied the lawns, only an "easterly" or driving, swirling shower could bully me off the rocking chair on that porch.

Service huts, college dorms, and apartment houses are not well suited to porch sitting in the rain. Somewhere along the way I decided that when I owned my own home I would have a porch (a patio today) so large as to be a challenge to even the severest of summer storms. So, many years ago, I laid a concrete slab floor behind my home. I bought a rocking chair—old, wooden, and high backed, in anticipation of the completed job. Next, the roof was put on. My "porch" was finished. It is long and it is deep, and it has an open railing.

Mike and Jeanne Piedmonte

Today, years later, a heavy, steady downpour is coming from a sky so black it looks as though it may be several miles thick with rain. And as I sit on my patio, I'm happy to say that the quiet, comfort, and coziness of being close to the rain still hasn't changed a bit. It still feels as good as I can remember it when I was a youngster.

And there's a bonus now; the rocking chair feels even better than it did years ago.

Tell-Tale "Lifestyle" Signs

You don't drive as much anymore after sunset

You are a big fan of television's TVLand Channel

You know that a Fox Trot is not something a fox does when it is in a hurry

You are always one of the first 20 people in church on any Sunday morning

You have decided, "the hell with Rogaine"

You know the words to sing-a-long songs from World War II

You love it that many books now come in large print editions

You use the term "hip," but it's more in conversations about surgery than in ones about trends

You go to more viewings than parties

You used to use the term "shacking up" to denote cohabitation

You think words like "chairperson" and "waitserver" are ridiculous

Your broker suggests a less aggressive portfolio

You used to sprinkle your clothes before ironing

You seldom iron anymore

You move your feet instead of your shoulders while dancing

You pay bills on time

You realize that you have become, or want to become, a "snowbird"

You go to shareowner meetings

You can't bring yourself to wear jeans to church

You can play the piano

You keep a leisure suit in the closet, "just in case they come back into style"

You are taking art courses

You carry a plastic rain bonnet in your purse

You wear a corporation pin that has stones in it

You work such part-time jobs as a bagger in a supermarket or as a funeral director assistant

You go food shopping with your wife

You go on bus trips to dinner shows

You vote in off-year elections

You drive a big Caddy, Grand Marquis, or Lincoln Towncar

You use the words ensure and depends—but they are usually capitalized

You stand in front of a mirror pushing loose skin around

You take most of the day to do what you used to do on your lunch hour

You've said that you would be wealthy if, over the years, you had kept half of all the "worthless junk" that you threw away or gave away

You are one of the first ones to leave wedding receptions and holiday parties

Grunts, Groans Will Break My Bones

When I was in high school, I could get through double coverage to drive for a layup. During the early years of marriage, I could get in 200 sit-ups and 100 push-ups during a single workout. In later years, I could shoot about 36 holes of golf or even get to first base on a slow grounder. But now I'm a senior citizen, and I can't even get out of a car without grunting.

Now don't get me wrong—this senior business hasn't sapped all my strength or agility. I can still twist the truth, raise the roof, push the envelope and pull my weight. And just watch me turn a corner, stretch a dollar and make ends meet. I've also become adept at exercising my rights, doing a double take and bending over backwards when necessary. It's just that I'll be darned if I can open a bag of potato chips.

There are some compensating advantages to my loss of strength and agility. I'm no longer expected to climb ladders in order to paint the shutters on the second floor, nor scramble around rooftops to retrieve errant balls that found their way into our spouting. I don't get under cars anymore, and I'm not asked to march over hill and dale. I especially like not carrying heavy bags or pushing stalled cars. And how did I ever get along without sit-down mowers and electric leaf blowers?

Yes, I know there are things senior citizens can do to stave off further loss of strength and agility, maybe even gain some back, but none of them seem to appeal to me.

Take yoga, for example, I understand that the word yoga comes from the Sanskrit word Yug, which is too close to the English word, Yuck, to suit me. Exercises with names like Stretching Dog, Corpse Pose, Seated Sun, and Alternate Triangle cause my spine to weaken even more than it already has.

I'm told weight training is the latest panacea for many a senior citizen's ills, and who am I to argue with the professionals? However, even the use of expressions like dumbells, free weights and bench presses scare me off. What rational person can get excited about the idea of "pumping iron" or "no pain, no gain?"

The question comes down to this: Is lifting weights for me? And a little voice inside me (I suspect it is actually the voice of a potential hernia not wishing to wrestle with the wall of my stomach for pop position) keeps saying "No! No!"

Some of the other suggestions for me to regain my strength and agility barely deserve mention. There's no way in the world I am about to take up line dancing, do anything that requires me to play any sort of games in a swimming pool, or participate in any activity in which I have to wear wheels, blades, or helmets.

But in rare moments of introspection, I have to admit I do miss the ability to push a sled or lift a grandchild over my head. And during these times I consider joining in the activities at the senior center, the local Y, or even the nearby community college.

But I don't. Everybody there is so darn old.

(This article first appeared in the Sun News, Myrtle Beach SC)

Straight Answers to 12 Important Retirement Questions

As card-carrying senior retirees with Social Security and Medicare cards to prove it, we are often approached by "working people" who are sometimes curious and sometimes desperate to know about important retirement issues. Below are twelve of the most commonly asked questions and our attempt to answer them.

Q. Why do seniors travel so much?

A. It is a nice way to get away from their children for a while.

Q. What do seniors do to keep busy?

A. This is a tough question because it requires a definition for the word, "busy." When working people say "busy," they generally mean starting the day with a high decibel alarm, a gulped-down breakfast, and a rage-filled commute to the workplace. And then it goes downhill fast after that with telephones, beepers, fax machines, computers, deadlines, Dilbert-type managers, and soccer practices. So the answer to this question is: seniors don't do anything to keep busy. Why the heck should we?

Q. "But how will I *fill* my day after I retire?" working people persist in knowing.

A. Buy a computer. You will never have enough time for anything else after that.

Q. Will I (working person) have enough money after I retire?

Mike and Jeanne Piedmonte

A. Yes. (This usually ends the conversation since the working people getting this optimistic response figure us to be totally senile and anxious to get as far away as possible. As a result, we seldom get the chance to explain that for the most part they are no longer working for the various levels of government. And that now most of their former tax dollars are not going into political coffers but into their own pockets.)

Q. I often hear seniors speak of an ailment called CRS but I cannot find it in any medical dictionary or on the Internet. What is this condition?

A. This is a very important question and we know the answer. We just can't seem to remember what it is right now.

Q. I often hear that one's sex drive diminishes as one gets older. Is this true?

A. This depends on which sex you are.

Q. Why are seniors sometimes so, well, rude?

A. It's not so much rudeness as it is self-centeredness. Be patient with these particular seniors. Constant pain and the realization that you *don't* want to live forever sometimes does this to people.

Q. We hear so much about saving enough for retirement years, especially with seniors living so much longer these days. Don't seniors become afraid of running out of money before they die?

A. Some seniors have this fear. However, many of today's seniors are even more fearful of dying before they run out of money.

Q. Now that both spouses are not working and are together a lot more, don't you get on each other's nerves?

A. Hell, yes.

Q. Don't seniors miss their workplace friends after they retire?

A. Of course, but this void only lasts until you get a life.

Q. How do you feel about relocating after you have retired?

A. That depends very much on how you felt about relocating while you were still working.

Q. What is the most important thing a senior retiree should know?

A. When it is that everyone has stopped listening to you.

Mike and Jeanne Piedmonte

The Early Bird Gets to Wait

One thing that I don't like about being a Senior Citizen is that it happened too early in my life. Almost as bad is the fact that this "early syndrome" has carried over into my senior years and now I'm early for everything

It wasn't always this way. In fact, I was some two weeks late arriving in this world.

And when my mother would tire of trying to rouse me for school, she would say that I would probably be late for my own viewing.

Like many other youngsters, I had little comprehension of time. It wasn't a finite quantity; there was plenty of it. What was the hurry? So I was often tardy for school, behind in handing in assignments, and late for meals, baths, and puberty.

As a young man, I was late for dates, exams, and practices. This all came in handy during my military service days. I never did hurry up and wait. And I must confess that I was a little late for my wedding.

But no more. Now that I'm a senior, I arrive at church before the lights are turned on. ("What better place to wait?" says my wife.)

Don't ask me why, but we arrive at the movie theater at 6:30 for the 7 p.m. showing. This is to make sure we get a good seat, even though we usually go to the movies on weekday nights when the theater is almost always empty.

So we wait and watch all those maddening attempts at entertainment, coupled with periodic admonitions to be quiet and to get our butts up to the refreshment stand. And then, when the coming attractions start, someone turns up the volume about 1500 decibels in case a jet should suddenly fly over head and we would miss the best dialogue bits from eight different upcoming movies.

Yes, I know we could avoid all this if we entered the theater at 7:10 p.m. But there's no sense sitting in the car in the parking lot all that time.

I arrive at garage sales, tag sales, yard sales and flea markets even before the dealers do. It's usually too dark to actually see what I'm purchasing, but I get there earlier than the pros—and that's what's important.

When I call for takeout pizza and I'm told it will be about 20 minutes, I get to the pizza shop in 10. So I wait, but I don't mind. It's a great place to meet other seniors who also are 10 to 15 minutes early. And I watch those young mothers and fathers who are picking up their pizzas 20 minutes later than they were supposed to.

Tradesmen who tell you that they will be at your house at 8 a.m. usually don't get there before 10 a.m. Tradesmen who tell you that they will be there at 10 a.m. usually don't get there until the next day. Does that stop seniors like myself from being ready at 7 a.m.? Be serious.

Airlines want you at the airport two hours ahead of schedule. To seniors, this is calling things way too close. What if there is a traffic jam on the way? What if there is an accident in any part of the airport? What if there are no parking spaces? What if it is a long way to the terminal? What if you have trouble at security? What if the plane is early?

Oh, there are lots of other instances (appointments with auto mechanics, reserved seats at plays and sporting events, among others) where I always seem to be early even though I know down deep it won't do me a bit of good. But what can I do? It's a senior thing.

Mike and Jeanne Piedmonte

I think my mother was wrong. I won't be late for my own viewing. That wouldn't be fair to all those senior friends of mine who will come long before the announced calling hours—so they can get in and out before it gets crowded.

(This article first appeared in the San Francisco Examiner)

Ten 'Why's' But Only One Answer

Putting together lists of 10 is big these days and for a long time we've wanted to take part in this media-driven entertainment form. However, not being experts in any particular field has long stifled our desire to share with the world any lists of Bests and Worsts. In all honesty, we can't write about the best clothing designers, moments in sports history, or movies of the past year.

However, our being Senior Citizens does qualify us to assemble the following list of Ten Things That We'll Be Damned If We Can Understand Why People Do.

No. 10 Why do people, when driving on city streets or on highways that are under construction, insist on passing you so they can wait at the next traffic light or merge sign in front of you instead of in back of you? Why do these people persist in swerving in front of you only to have to slam on their brakes? Where do they think they are going in a line of traffic a mile long? Are these people born idiots or were they put on earth by space aliens to test our endurance?

No. 9 Why are receptionists at doctors' and dentists' offices so diligent about calling to remind you of your 1 p.m. appointment, but *never* call you to say the doctor is running two hours late and that there is no sense coming in before 3 p.m? Do these people think we have nothing better to do with those two hours than read gastrointestinal and tooth implant brochures?

No. 8 Why are males so uncomfortable in Mens Rooms that they often will not even completely dry their hands (or even wash them sometimes) in their haste to leave? Why will males of all ages stare blankly at the wall in front of them as if some mental TV were turned on? Why will good friends, even fathers and sons, barely acknowledge knowing one another until out that door?

No. 7 Why do people who work in offices and answer the phone for others often say, "May I ask who is calling?" Is it the intent of the Someone answering the phone to find out if you are worthy to speak with The Person? Will The Person not speak to you if he or she realizes you are someone who is not important enough to bother with?

No. 6 Why do sportscasters carry on as if it matters who wins today's game, or next week's playoff, or next month's series or Superbowl? Other than the "sports family" of broadcasters, players, coaches, and assorted associates, all of whom depend on these games to provide their paychecks, who *really* cares besides the gamblers? Isn't professional sports today as if Microsoft were playing IBM and you're not a stockholder in either company?

No. 5 Why do people dislike foods they've never eaten, books they've never read, or shows they've never seen? How does one summarily dismiss all seafood, some religions, and most radio talk shows? Is it in many people's minds really enough that one has tasted an oyster and didn't like it, read a chapter of a particular bible and didn't understand it or heard three minutes of a talk show and didn't agree with the host? Why this rush to judgment? Why this paucity of patience and absence of adventure? Why at a time when society, as a whole, is capable of accepting a "giant leap for mankind" are we, as individuals, unwilling to sample tofu?

No 4 Why do women who have been in the company of one another for several hours at a social gathering find the need to start an entirely new topic of discussion upon departing, thereby adding an additional 20 minutes to the process of saying goodbyes? Are such topics kept in reserve for these parting moments?

No. 3 Why do people take children to see R-rated movies? Don't these people know that implicit in R-rated movies is graphic violence or sex? What parents *want* their nine-year old to see blasting bombs or bouncing boobs? Don't these people have any sense at all?

No. 2 Why do people on Internet bulletin boards discuss topics irrelevant to the board? With thousands of different boards to choose from, why do we have to see on a "books" board a discussion on why Canadians don't like Americans? Or in a "genealogy" board, why a treatise on the responsibility to vote? Or in a "humor" board, why a religious chain letter? Is subject matter beyond the scope of Internerds?

No. 1 Why do people bother to read these Lists of 10? Have we no lives to the point we need someone to tell us which movies we should have liked or which celebrities were the worst dressed, or even why people do the things they do? On the other hand, why do people bother to compile these silly lists. Well, at least for this "Why?" there is a clear and concise answer. Money. Now if we could just get more people to buy this book…

Mike and Jeanne Piedmonte

These Arch Supports Were Made for Walking

Go around anywhere in the country on most mornings and what you will see are seniors out for their daily walks.

You don't have to look very hard to notice that all these senior walkers are not alike. In fact, since we've purposely excluded seniors who are being walked by their dogs, we can categorize senior walkers into the following loose categories:

The Pro. These Senior Citizens are strong out of the gate and keep up this pace for the duration of their walks. However, speed is not their main focus; determination to prevail is. You can see this determination in the starry stare and the forward thrust of their bodies against nature's elements. If you come across a pro on the go, remember that you may see him or her, but they may be looking right past you. So get the heck out of their way!

Same Sex Pair. These pairs are almost always senior females (senior males usually don't walk in pairs unless they are with their wives or they are on golf courses). Same-sex pairs are in no hurry. Walking is just a good excuse for chatting which constitutes the bulk of the energy expended.

Married Pair. If you see a senior man and woman walking together and they are not speaking to one another, you can bet they are a married pair. Married pairs walk at a cautionary, moderate pace. Unlike the previous two categories, Married Pairs are friendly and will always greet fellow walkers. After all, they have to have someone to speak to.

The Athlete. These good seniors are easy to spot because of what they wear. Even though they may not actually be more athletic or even healthier than the rest of us seniors, they sure do look like they are. They wear caps with well-rounded brims, sleek-looking sunglasses and nylon warm-up suits. And, of course, the best of walking shoes. Occasionally, you'll see an Athlete in a spandex outfit but since this is intended to be a humorous essay, we won't go there.

The Logistics Walker(s). Also known as the Practical People, these good seniors may be solitary or in pairs. When they first embark on their walk, they have their arms free and swing away. If you were to see them on their return, they would be carrying bags of groceries or merchandise. They will explain, "My goodness, there is no sense taking a walk just for the sake of walking, may as well do something useful."

The Obvious Snowbird. These senior walkers go winter walking in the warmer climates as if they are still up in the "cold states." They can be seen bundled up against vicious 50 and 60 degree temperatures wearing heavy jackets, woolen hats, and ski mittens.

But regardless of which category our senior walkers fall into, they all do have one thing in common: They want to stay healthy enough to enjoy many more walks. God bless them.

Mike and Jeanne Piedmonte

Important Tips for Touring Seniors

Many Senior Citizens these days are using tour companies to facilitate traveling to Europe, Asia, and other destinations. The following "tour tips" are some of the items and situations seniors should be aware of and prepare for on a trip to Europe, for example.

First of all, you are not getting forgetful and missing a day. Day One of your tour is not really the first day of your tour. Day One is the day you leave for the airport, wait several hours as you go through security and experience schedule delays, make any necessary commuter connections, finally board your overseas flight, wait some more on the tarmac, and then spend the rest of the day or evening trying to get some sleep.

Day Two begins with you being awakened by a middle-of-the-night sunrise and a flight attendant with all the congeniality of a hospital night-shift nurse. On Day Last, you usually catch an early morning flight home and spend almost the entire day squeezed into an economy seat with many other similarly positioned and pooped seniors who will either want to sleep or talk the entire flight.

Speaking of sleep, seniors should expect to get most of their sleep while on the tour bus. Tour guides usually call for early starts, especially on days that you are going from one destination to another. This always seems to entail getting luggage outside your hotel room door and having breakfast before the light of day. These early starts are necessary to allow time to stop at gift shops between various sightseeing stops. So even on the bus the best you can hope for are some catnaps.

Tour guides are professional people. To become one, tests have to be taken, licenses granted, several languages spoken, and history learned. However, the most important thing a tour guide must be able to do is count. Take any tour with an abundance of seniors on it and every time the bus stops, even for a traffic light it seems, the tour guide will trudge up the aisle, counting heads and patiently waiting for the tour clown to demand that if anyone is missing they should raise their hand. Even though tour guides don't have a license to kill, it's still a good idea to stay out of their way most of the time.

Local guides are experts in their geographical area or specific subject and on the use of umbrellas. In order to keep the tour group small enough so everyone can hear, local guides walk fast enough so that at least 80 percent of the seniors cannot keep up no matter how hard they try. These tardy seniors' only contact with their local guide is their viewing of the guide's umbrella as it bobs up and down like a mast of a sailing ship as it winds through the turbulent Straits of Tourists. If you are one of the latecomers, don't worry. The guides' talks always last long enough so that the entire tour group is there in time to tip them.

Photo stops usually last four to five minutes. Gift shop stops on the other hand last about forty to fifty minutes. Even this generous amount of time may be extended if one of the senior ladies sprains or breaks a leg in her haste to disembark the bus too quickly. Be certain that this injured senior is not you! This poor woman's only hope is that she was one of the last to exit the bus, or she may be trampled and spat upon by the other senior ladies eager to buy souvenirs and gifts for their grandchildren.

The delicate subject of natural functions has to be addressed, at least in a minimal way, in any piece on senior touring for two important reasons: One, tour schedules are usually quite rigid and Two, the natural function schedules of seniors are usually quite erratic, to say the least. So it's well to know that the tour's schedule of early starts and late dinners will soon result in the seniors' toilet schedules becoming more and more unnatural.

There are many more tips that we could pass on to novice and even experienced senior travelers, but the mail has just arrived and it contains a fresh batch of colorful brochures from several tour companies. We just love reading these things.

Why a "Happy Anniversary" Is Easier Said Than Done

Maybe when we were younger, the buying of an anniversary card (or get well or birthday wish, etc.) was a simple, pleasant experience. But now that we are senior women it seems that these purchases have become a more traumatic and time-consuming task for most of us.

We don't simply mosey up to a selection of greeting cards and easily find one that meets the exacting demands placed on it by the somber or joyous occasion we wish to commemorate. No, indeed, choosing that "just right' greeting card requires a special mental and physical condition.

Mentally, we must be attuned to the occasion and to the recipient of the card. Matching the card and its message to the recipient and the occasion is, after all, what sending a card is all about, right? Physically, we must have the stamina required for the tedious task of reading through dozens of greeting verse and prose in search of the "one and only" that expresses our sentiments exactly.

Regardless of the occasion, it seems that most of us go through that same decision-making process in selecting a card. This process takes us through about ten steps, which go something like this:

1. First, we have to know the tone of the card and the type of message we want to convey to, for example, the newlyweds or the bereaved (or in some cases, the bereaved newlyweds). Do we want our greeting to be serious, mushy, humorous, outrageous, somber,

reflective, inspiring, terse, or wordy? Should our message be in the form of prose or verse? In other words, we first develop some general sense of what we want.

2. Having decided on this, we next consider the size of the card and the price we want to pay. (As you know, greeting cards come in sizes ranging from wallet size to wall mural proportions.) Also, size and cost go hand-in-hand. On the other hand, well written messages and/or borrowed quotes from famous poets and philosophers cost no more than punch line puns.

3. At this step, we know more specifically what we want. Now comes the hard part—finding time to buy a card. For some reason, nobody ever goes shopping just to buy a greeting card. This purchase is always squeezed in with several other chores and is relegated to being handled during such other activities as paying a bill, or shopping for something else—"And, oh yes, I must pick up a Father's Day card, too," we say to ourselves.

4. The decision as to where to buy our card is fairly easy—the discount store, supermarket, drug store, gift shop, department store—wherever we'll get the best discount. About the only place, it seems, that we can't presently buy a greeting card is at a bank, and I'm sure that's in the works. And, let's face it, most of us are not into e-mailing greeting cards. There is just some mail that requires opening an envelope.

5. We are, finally, at the card rack. Now for the actual physical act of selecting and purchasing a card. There is a certain approach to systematically doing this. We first look over the entire selection at least once. This perusal involves picking off the shelf and opening a

couple of dozen cards to read the inside message and then returning each card to the rack. (This step would be less time consuming if only we stuck to our original goal of picking out, say, an anniversary card, but most of us also will examine cards in other categories. For example, we'll also look at humorous birthday or thoughtful thinking-of-you cards.)

6. Having quickly reviewed the array of cards, we are now ready for the heart of our assignment—picking a specific card. Here most of us use the process of elimination. This involves going back over the entire selection and again opening and closing cards, but this time holding on to those which are close to what we are looking for. Each time we find a better one, we put one or two of the previous "closies" back on the shelf.

7. When we've been through the rack a second (or perhaps a third) time, we hopefully have a couple of cards that we've decided deserve our further approval. We eventually narrow it down to a card of our choice! But, darn, on second thought, we don't *really* like it. So we return it, too, to the rack and often are left empty handed—only now the store closes in an hour or, our patience is half shot, or our meter has expired.

8. We go through the entire selection once more, this time zeroing in on that special card with less finickiness and with more determination to get on with a selection. Once more we come up with a card that even though wins the elimination contest, again loses its appeal at the last second.

9. By now, a mild form of panic has set in. We have taken to checking our watch every couple of minutes and are on the verge of going to another store (and another entire selection) when we have the time later. But we break out in a rash at the thought of going this whole process again.

10. So, in the grip of despair, we return to the card we originally chose without bothering to reread it this time. We decide the card comes close enough to what we want to say. So, for the last time, we remove the card from the rack.

Now, if only we could find the envelope that goes with the card.

Who Put Up the 'Help Wanted' Sign?

Let's be honest about it, ladies. Our retired husbands can be annoying when they think they are being helpful.

My first experience with this occurred about a week after Mike retired. I had just returned from grocery shopping. He met me in the kitchen and proudly said, "Look at what I did for you." And with a grand gesture and a loud "taa daah" he showed me how he had arranged all my spice and condiment containers in alphabetical order. "Now you'll know exactly where everything is without having to search for it anymore,"

I was expecting—and dreading—this moment. I had been forewarned by many other wives that there would be a time, usually soon after his retirement that the now work-idled husband announces, "I've been looking around the house and there are a lot of things that I can help you with now that I have the time."

In addition to the fact that we wives usually don't need—or want—the help (we've been doing just fine for these many years, thank you), it's also that these well-meaning retiree husbands try to be helpful in the only way they can be—the *male* way.

From my many conversations with other senior wives, here are some of the unasked for but well intended helpful male attempts that lead directly to female annoyance. Do these sound familiar?

"Need any help?" he asks, knowing that we are expecting company for dinner.

"Yes, you can set the table," you reply sweetly.

"Okay, will do. Soon as I finish what I'm doing. Only take a minute."

(20 minutes later)

"Did you set the table yet?" you ask.

"Not yet. Forgot I had something else, too. Be right there."

"Well the company will be here in half an hour!" you say, a lot less sweetly.

"Relax. We have plenty of time."

*

Helpful retired husbands absolutely do not believe in going from point A to point B without first getting deeply into the logistics of the trip. "Can't you wait until tomorrow and we can go by way of the gas station and cleaners and make it all in one trip?" he wants to know.

"I don't want to wait until tomorrow. I have *other* things to do tomorrow," you say in a voice somewhere between a shout and a scream.

*

"Want me to make the bed today" he asks.

Now, any woman who would say "yes" to this question should be immediately committed. Rare is the man who knows enough to put the blankets and sheets on evenly on both sides of a bed. Or to put a bedspread on correctly.

*

Information gathering is another area where well-meaning retired husbands do not make the grade. For example, a new neighbor has just moved in so retired husband volunteers to introduce us—and to find out as much as possible about them, you think

"Seems like a nice fellow. His name is Tom," retired husband says.

"He say where he works?" you ask.

"No. Something with computers."

"They have children?"

"He didn't mention any."

"What's his wife's name?"

"He didn't mention her."

"Where are they from?"

"Don't know. I did find out that he is a pro football fan. Mostly we talked about the Eagles and the weather. Seems like a nice guy, like I said."

"Didn't you want to know *anything* about his family?" you ask incredulously.

"Figure if he wanted me to know he would have told me," he responds with typical male logic.

*

You would think that a retired guy, with all the time in the world, wouldn't feel the need to always take shortcuts when doing things—especially when trying to be helpful. Ever watch your spouse vacuum? Don't. Men do not seem to understand that rooms have corners (unless they are mitering something). Ever watch him clean a mirror in the house? Don't. And why is it, they can't replace a centerpiece in the center of a table, or close a bureau drawer all the way, or put clothes into a hamper?

*

For the sake of brevity, we'll overlook the annoyances associated with helping to make meals together (Where do you keep the bagels? Isn't a cup equal to two teaspoons? So what's your problem, it's a self-cleaning oven, isn't it?)

*

And helping with the laundry. Don't you bleach colored loads, too? They are both small loads, why not just put them together into one big load? Why do you have to fold everything?

*

And so, ladies, this leaves one last really helpful thing that our retiree husbands try their hardest to be helpful with—improving our sex lives. Need I comment?

As I said before, our retired husbands mean well and we appreciate that. But men and women are different, as we well know. And besides, I don't recall ever posting on the refrigerator door a "Help Wanted" sign.

TELL-TALE "MENTAL" SIGNS

You occasionally complain that you never so much as closed your eyes all night

You *know* that manufacturers are putting bottle caps on more tightly each year

You think a motherboard is a woman with no interests other than her children

You pay attention to wrinkle removal cream commercials

You get a second opinion on everything from open heart surgery to lawn mower repairs

You realize that crows feet aren't just on crows

You think that everyone drives too damn fast

You wish a boom box were a self-detonating explosive device

You tell youngsters that a potbelly is one of the rewards of a good life

Your mid-life crisis is just a distant memory

You know that contract bridge doesn't require a lawyer

You are told that it's "cute" when you and your spouse hold hands

You refuse to pay the price for a first-run movie

You've quit reading the "Engagements" page of your local newspaper

You don't notice that you are wearing non-matching plaids

You forget to take your "doggie bag" when you leave the restaurant

You are told that your head has become thicker than your hair

Your insurance man stops sending you a calendar for the upcoming year

You realize that nobody knows how to raise kids anymore

You receive more solicitations from cemetery companies

You realize you trust the government less now, but rely on it more

You worry about the fifth day of a five-day weather forecast

You sometimes refer to someone as "an old fool" and you've been called one, too

You can't believe you ever *liked* snow

You think that a "fax" is a phonetic spelling of "facts"

You don't know the difference between "snail mail" and "e-mail"

You own a shoe shine kit

You wonder how gray you would be without your regular trips to the beauty salon

You feel "entitled" to entitlements

You will never forgive Ted Turner for colorizing the movie, *It's a Wonderful Life*

You turn to the obituaries page first when reading the morning newspaper

You can't seem to remember jokes anymore

You realize that housework doesn't seem as important as it once did

You seldom go anywhere in the evening without first anticipating what time you will be home

You liked it a lot better when all the numbers you had to remember were your street address and phone number.

Rock A Bye Senior

I'm told that the day I was born I slept through the night.

I know that as a youngster in New York City, I slept through the constant sounds of police sirens, fire alarms, and the clickity clack of the "els." I could sleep full or hungry, tired or wired, sitting or standing up. As a teen I could sleep through the shrill call of alarm clocks and entire classes of lively lectures. Later, reveille and muster were no match for my somnolence.

After marriage, I could sleep through labor pains (if not poked by my sometimes inconsiderate wife). The cries and screams of babies didn't jar me from my dreams (again though, with the poking to contend with), nor did the sounds of boom boxes or keys turning in the lock way after midnight curfew arouse me.

My mother-in-law used to say that she didn't close her eyes all night and I used to think that was quite an exaggeration. But now that I'm a Senior Citizen, I find that the din of a garbage truck two blocks away awakens me. Our neighbor two houses away opening his garage door bolts me upright. And the cat jumping from the couch to the floor two rooms away does not go unheard by me

I try to be optimistic, and therefore constructive, about these extra hours of wakefulness that I have at my disposal. I use this time to "catch up" and to get things done. I see a lot of old movies that I either missed or wanted to see again. Letterman and Leno I feel kindred to. Coupons get clipped, books and magazines get read, mail gets written and web sites get visited.

These dark hours are also good for visiting. Sometimes I travel as far back as the Depression, World War II, and high school.

But these dark hours are even better for regretting. Could haves…should haves…would haves…constantly pry loose from my brain. I should never have started smoking. I should have watched my diet more. I should have taken better care of my teeth…

But these dark hours are best of all for worrying. I just can't seem to worry as well during the day as I can during those really early morning hours. Too many distractions, I guess.

Not only do I have more time for worries, but they are also much clearer. Sometimes my worries can reach the level of pure angst. I can visualize natural and man-made disasters with clarity. I can experience medical emergencies and unfortunate accidents before they happen. I can unearth financial ruin beneath every economic boom.

And in these wee hours, I also have the time to worry about the Big Picture Questions—Where is our society heading? What is the future role of NATO? When will this war on terrorism end? How will our kids spend their inheritances?

All this worrying and otherwise occupying myself during these dark, early hours does, however, have one big advantage. It frees me to use my daytime hours in more productive and rewarding activities, like taking naps.

Successful Retirement Depends on Having Attitude

While reading an article about Social Security, I learned that about 77 million baby boomers will begin retiring during this decade. I find this to be shocking news. Not because of the obvious financial effects, about which the politicians are already worrying (or at least they say they are worrying). No, my concern is that in the very near future there will be many men and women who do not have the "bad ass" attitude that they will need to enjoy being retired.

Studies indicate that the act of retiring is one of life's most traumatic experiences, right up there with death, marriage, and eating cold pizza. As an experienced retiree, I can tell you the "retirement experience" will continue to be traumatic if you don't follow some important rules regarding your attitude.

The biggest mistake newly retired people of both sexes make is thinking and behaving as if they are still employed. They continue to think that they are still players in the myriad and on-going plots and subplots of the work environment, that they still must justify a salary, hourly wage, or company profit, that they still "must get along" with egomaniac bosses, pompous bureaucrats, or obnoxious coworkers.

So listen up good, you young'ns who will be retiring soon, or have recently retired: *You are no longer a "worker without an attitude."* I don't care if you were a CEO of a large company, an office suit, a union laborer, a small business owner, or a member of the clergy; a "worker

97

Mike and Jeanne Piedmonte

without an attitude" is what you had to be in order to last long enough to formally retire.

Yes, I know that putting aside this concept is easier said than put into practice, so here are six important rules for being a "retiree with a bad-ass" attitude:

Rule 1. Don't create work for yourself around your house or yard. You are truly your own boss now, and nobody can create work but you— and yes, this includes your spouse.

For example, don't put fertilizer on the lawn. It only makes the grass grow faster, and you'll have to cut it more often. You will probably harvest more weeds than vegetables from any garden, so grow an attitude instead. Don't go looking for projects to do. Projects split and create new ones themselves without any help from you. What's important here is that you have an attitude and not goals.

Rule 2. Do things right the first time. I know this runs contrary to everything you ever learned at work, but if you are retired and have a bad ass attitude you can be an expert on most matters. And since no boss-given appraisal is going to affect your fixed-income pension or social security, you can take an interest in how and why you are doing something.

Rule 3. Never go shopping with your spouse if you can possibly help it. For a retiree with a b-a attitude, shopping with his or her spouse will be as enjoyable (and as unnecessary) as going on a business trip with the boss used to be. No, there is no way a trip to the mall can be a win-win situation with each of you having different agendas but the same expense account. Besides, it is wise not to clash with someone who also has a b-a attitude.

Rule 4. Take vacations. You are now entitled to 52 weeks a year vacation, so take them. Just because you are retired, you shouldn't make the mistake of thinking you do not need a vacation. You will, in fact, need them more than ever because you now will now be busier than you were while working. Is there anyone who hasn't heard a retiree say, "I'm so busy. I don't know when I found time to work." There is a great second reason, which is that going on vacation while you are retired means not coming back to two weeks of work that has been piling up on you.

Rule 5. Speak up, speak out! Hey, your days of having to be passive during a budget meeting or quiet during a boring seminar are over. Now you can call your senators, write letters to the editor, reprimand anyone, and even scold your grandchildren. With a little luck, you'll overhear some whisper about you, "Talk about an attitude!"

Rule 6. Keep yourself healthy so you can have a long retirement. A long retirement gives you the last laugh on the system. Think of it as a life-end bonus that you really earned.

(This article first appeared in The Morning Call, Allentown PA)

Mike and Jeanne Piedmonte

It's Not What You Know, It's What You Understand

Now that I'm a Senior Citizen, the things that I know now are so different from what I knew when I was a child, or even a young man.

As with so many things, this change in knowledge occurred so slowly that I paid no attention except, perhaps, for an occasional and brief sigh. But now that the sighs come with more frequency and fall deeper into my lungs, I am aware that some of the "then" and "now" knowledge varies greatly. For example,

Then, I could tell you the batting averages of half the ball players in the National League. Now that I'm a senior, I can tell you the exact numbers of my PSA and cholesterol. (What really hurts is that my cholesterol numbers would bring many a young ball player today a hefty bonus.)

Then, I knew the location of every swimming hole and fishing spot in the area. Now, I can tell you the location of every men's room in every mall and restaurant in my area. And just as I couldn't wait to get to those swimming holes as a kid, these days I can barely make it to the men's rooms.

Then I knew that a tricycle consisted of two small back wheels connected to a larger front wheel by a tubular bar upon which sat a triangular seat. Today I know that triglycerides are chemical compounds consisting of three molecules of fatty acid combined with one molecule of glycerol.

Then, I would drive my old teachers crazy with my antics. Now that I'm old, I drive young drivers crazy with my antics.

Then, as a young man, I knew by heart the phone numbers of many a pretty woman with whom I could go dancing—cut a rug, as we used to call it. Speaking of cutting, I now can call the number of my heart surgeon without looking it up. And nowadays, the only pretty young ladies who call me by my first name are employed in the doctors' offices or in the blood labs.

Then, I used to go with dates to county fairs where I would measure my strength by ringing a bell. Now I go with my wife to health fairs and measure my blood pressure by holding still.

Then, I knew all the ingredients to make a great mixed drink. Now, I know all the active ingredients in my prescriptions.

Then, I would jog five miles a day. Now I log that many miles going to and from the bathroom each night.

Then, with a lot of grunting, I could bench press my weight. Now it takes the same amount of grunting to press myself out of bed.

Then, I never worried about the effects of what I was doing. Now, I always worry about the side effects of what I am taking.

Then, I understood engines and gasoline. Now, I understand fiber and flatulence.

And the list could go on …

But I want any young readers and, in particular, serious persons of middle age, to please take lightly these "now" and "then" comparisons. Sure, the things I know now are not always as enjoyable as the things I knew then. But there is one particular joyful upside to old age that is frequently overlooked and it's this: Much of what I only *knew* then, I *understand* now.

Mike and Jeanne Piedmonte
(This article first appeared in The Morning Call, Allentown PA)

Worrying

"Worry" is a word that deserves more screening
'Cause not everyone knows its full meaning.

Like anything else, whether you're amateur or pro
Worry is something you've learned to know.

Amateur worriers fuss and fret and then let go
But pro worriers hang in there, going toe-to-toe.

When you are young and insecure your worries,
Like you, are immature.

And then comes the years of being a high roller
Followed by those of pushing a stroller.

And worries now include your kids and your job
And what you might do to your boss, the big blob.

Then, unexpectedly, the kids are on their own
And you and your spouse are suddenly alone.

So for a while you fulfill that requirement
That each of you enjoy your retirement

But by now you've had a lifetime of accumulating woes.
Quietly, you've left the amateur ranks and joined the pros.

So get on the fast track and be in a hurry

Mike and Jeanne Piedmonte

To go for the quest of championship worry?
Or call on your inner strength and
What some call faith.

And look and laugh at how little you gain
From all your worry and its pointless pain.

Till finally you say, "it's out of my hands so get out of
my head.
I don't want to be 'too late smart and too soon dead.'"

(Authors' note: Darned if we're going to worry about
what bad poets we are.)

How to Spot the Endangered Grayhaired Snowbird

Just as the swallows return each spring to San Juan Capistrano, so each spring do the Grayhaired Snowbirds migrate back to the "cold states."

The Snowbirds can be seen in large numbers following ancient migratory routes along all major interstates. Mostly they travel in RVs, uncustomized vans, and large sedans as many of them figuratively fly back to the roosts of their families and friends.

Unfortunately, in recent years the number of Snowbirds returning northward has been steadily diminishing as many of this species are choosing to bask year-round in the sun and sand and foregoing the long trip back to the Cold States. As a result, the Grayhaired Snowbirds are fast becoming an endangered species.

Unlike some other endangered species, the Grayhaired Snowbirds are not dangerous to society. In fact, these birds still have many useful functions that are desperately needed in the Cold States. Among these are sitting for the grandchildren, volunteering for myriad causes, and keeping the local medical professions highly profitable, to name just a few.

As with any endangered species, the Grayhaired Snowbirds must be protected and nourished by the younger citizens of the Cold States so that these flighty birds might remain an important link in their social-economic environmental chain. Perhaps then they might be persuaded to continue to nest in the Cold States, joining their more hearty relatives, the Fourwalled Home Pigeons who thrive in the north's snow banks and blustery winter winds.

Unlike such common birds as the swallow, or robin, or bluejay, the Grayhaired Snowbird is not usually easily identifiable because of its many varieties. Here then are a few helpful hints at recognizing various species:

Some walk with a slight tilt as a result of spending too much time on sandy beaches.

Some speak slowly and deliberately, and may even have acquired a slight drawl.

Some will suddenly and for no apparent reason swing at an imaginary golf ball with an imaginary golf club.

Male Snowbirds can often be heard discussing route numbers and the shortest migration routes.

Most species can and will discuss at great length the rooms, rates, and continental breakfasts of the various motel chains.

Most species are often spotted shopping at local malls dressed in their brightly colored jogging outfits.

If you should spot a Grayhaired Snowbird, be gentle so as not to scare it off. Social researchers are just now beginning to understand why these birds migrate to warmer climates and how each year they instinctively seem to know how far their flight has to be to avoid the harsh winters of the Cold States. But much more research is needed.

In a recent study regarding Grayhaired Snowbird winter destinations, several of these birds were asked about how they determined their final destinations. One replied, "I tie a snow shovel to the roof of my auto. The first time I stop for gas and someone asks, 'What's that thing on top of your car?' I know I've gone far enough."

Sound Off

I can't shout the way I used to.

When I was a youngster I could call anyone from as far away as the horizon. I gave warnings whole city blocks away over the din of peak traffic. I could outhowl any kid in junior high school. And when it came to cheering at athletic events, I had, in all modesty, no equal.

At football games I could scream for hours. I would sit through baseball doubleheaders and come out as strong in voice as when I entered, bent on hooting at umpires and badgering opposing players.

I could imitate Tarzan's mighty yell as I descended from tree top to river on my rope of vine. With loud verbosity, I could stream forth profundities of comic book and movie heroes.

In high school and then at college my voice kept pace with my growing body. At games I could be heard clearly over thousands of chanting students and frenzied alumni.

During this vocal period of my life I also could shout down most girls during those all-too-serious arguments in those all-too-serious years.

During my service days, I developed a boatswain-like bass which issued orders that could be heard from stem to stern aboard a carrier even during rough winds and choppy seas. Ashore, I was a one-man Mitch Miller Sing-a-Long group, in volume anyway. My mating call was a rollicking gusty song, each note sung loud and clear.

Even after I settled down I could still out shout feuding neighbors, lip it with angry coworkers, and bark at backyard dogs. When reason failed, I could scold children, and I have even been known to raise my voice at my good wife.

But no longer. Lately it seems that I'm much too short winded to shout and yell as I used to. My voice cracks and creaks and my throat strains and swells.

Really, I don't mind that time has added a few extra pounds nor do I particularly mind it taking some of my hair and graying the rest. But I must confess that it has made me gruff knowing that I'm not as able to express myself.

TELL-TALE "SEXUAL" SIGNS

You don't joke about sex, but sex is a joke

You can't wait until your spouse loses his sex drive, too

You still enjoy sex. You're just not sure why

Your golf drive is the only drive you've lost

Your spouse no longer worries that you may be "running around"

Your gynecologist has stopped asking you if it hurts when you have intercourse

You start telling your spouse that quality is better than quantity

Your idea of kinky is a muscle cramp

You find yourself more concerned with your prostate than with your partner

"Early to bed, early to rise" now refers to sleep

You sometimes wish that someone thought of you as a "dirty old man"

You lament that climaxes now only occur in movies and books

You know that when seniors talk of the "blue pill" they are not talking about an antidepressant

You can live without sex but not without shopping

You have traded in a "matinee" for an "EARLY BIRD SPECIAL!!!"

A Senior's Sex Fantasy
Shouldn't Be A Russian Novel

There is a lot of concern amongst some seniors about sex fantasies. Mainly, they are worried because they no longer have them.

"I never daydream anymore of making it with movie stars, or athletes, or even villains," they say. "I no longer fantasize about being bound and gently but firmly had," they lament. "I don't ever even think about size anymore," they admit. "Am I too old to have occasional titillating thoughts?" they ask worriedly.

To these seniors we say, put your minds at ease. You no doubt are as abnormal and oversexed as everyone else. You probably have just forgotten how to go about having an honest-to-goodness sex fantasy.

Also, unless you were lucky enough to be born with a naturally dirty mind, fantasies do take a bit of doing. After, all, you have to give it *some* thought. And a quality Hollywood-type sex fantasy can be a bit of a production problem.

Okay, so you are one of those seniors who have not been able to conjure up anything that turns you on lately. Or, you've only been able to turn out a series of "B" grade mental flicks. Don't get depressed. Instead, follow these few simple but effective suggestions:

You could, of course, watch some X-rated films. These would turn out a couple of scenarios for you and you could be well on your way. But you would feel sleazy and, besides, that would be copping out. You want to develop, write, produce, direct, and act in your own fantasy. Good for you!

When writing your sex fantasy, use a pencil in case you want to erase. And use lined paper. Seniors who are writing sex fantasies have a tendency to write uphill for some reason. Lined paper will help keep you straight.

Do not attempt to write your sex fantasy while seated at your kitchen table while having your morning coffee, or while seated in your dentist's waiting room, or while sitting in traffic. Times and locations such as these, let's face it, do not lend themselves toward fantasizing on the joys of the body.

Write your fantasy with a familiar location setting— select places that you have been to and know fairly well. For example, if in your scenario you are making it with an athlete, don't attempt to go "on location" to a locker room shower, penalty box, or dugout if you have never been in any of these. If you feel the desire to be "tied down" make it to a bedpost, not to a goal post.

Avoid subplots. You should be developing a nice simple fantasy, not a Russian novel with several intricate and interwoven stories going on at the same time. And while on the subject of plots—keep your sex fantasy moving along. Don't dally with philosophical or political nuances, for example. Instead, proceed happily along to a successful conclusion, or climax, if you will.

A senior's sex fantasy should not involve more than two or three people. More than this gets unwieldy and even the best of senior imaginations may get bogged down in trying to keep straight who is doing what to whom.

Keep your sex fantasy to yourself until you have developed, written, and edited your work. Only now are you ready for candlelight action. Also do not collaborate with anyone on your fantasy. While this may work well for Broadway musicals, two seniors arguing about what positions should be taken and when will take much of the fun out of your literary creation.

With these helpful hints, any Senior Citizen should be able to throw off any remaining fears he or she may have about not being able to come up with a sex fantasy tailored to his or her own latent libido.

Now comes the fun of giving the term "senior moment" a whole new meaning.

Mike and Jeanne Piedmonte

A Flexible Look At Senior Sex

There is the myth that Senior Citizens have little or no interest in sex. However, as we seniors know, this simply is not true. Our interest in sex has not diminished. What has diminished, however, is our agility, our dexterity, our athletic abilities. Heck, even our endurance.

When we were young, we used to joke that there were 57 sexual positions (since the sexual revolution of the '60s, there are probably a lot more now). Regardless, many of us seniors feel lucky just to be able to move in 57 positions, yet alone participate in sex acts at the same time.

Put another way, sex, if it is to be done right, has become too darn vigorous! How can a senior consider a "roll in the hay" when it's all we can do to roll out of bed. How can a senior have grunting sex in the back seat of a car when it takes the same amount of grunting just to get out of the front seat. How can a senior woman go "all out" when she can't get herself into a frilly nightie.

Okay, we are being blunt here so let's consider the problems that some sexual positions present to Senior Citizens. The Missionary Position requires the male partner to practically do pushups and stomach exercises at the same time. This is expected from senior men who can't even push themselves away from the dinner table? The Woman on Top Position would have the senior woman straddling her partner. This, from many senior women who have difficulty getting up from the hopper? The Standing Position requires both partners to stand for what could seem like ages when you have bad knees or need a hip replacement. And many more erotic positions entail both partners in Kama Sutra gymnastic positions. I mean, come on, this from people who need to do warm up exercises just to put on our socks or fasten our bras?

On the positive side, there are a couple of advantages to both sexes once sex had been relegated to the status of a second class activity. Here's a few that quickly come to mind:

The only size that matters now is the one of your waist.

You can finally quit having to be romantic.

Lust is too much work to bother with.

There are a lot fewer arguments.

Separate beds don't sound all that bad.

And (drum roll) it's now possible to be merry without all that *mess.*

Mike and Jeanne Piedmonte

Three "Secret" Senior Male Erogenous Zones

Ladies, the time has come, and perhaps not a moment too soon, to discuss some important sensual tips to arouse your senior male's sexual passions.

Much has already been written in the form of manuals, learned essays, instruction kits, pictorial reviews, how-to books, and out-and-out pornographic materials on the art of peaking a senior male's frenzy, having him reach a pulsating pitch, and having him attain an erupting explosion of ecstasy.

Offhand, you might think that everything possible to say on the esoteric subject of senior male erogenous zones has already been explored. So, ladies, here is a big bonus for having purchased this book—three more little known erogenous areas that will arouse the amour of your senior male.

Where are these "secret" areas of the male anatomy? How do you know these particular spots are really erogenous zones? How do you use them to stimulate and seduce him? Let's examine each separately and give each the special attention it deserves.

The Bridge of the Nose. Reference to the erotic potential of nose bridges predates the Kama Sutra in ancient Indian and Arabic literature. Yama Ujjain in one of his early works speaks of the "blissful and enchanting nose hump." Some scholars even believe the wearing of masks was originally designed to cover this sensuous bridge and prevent female ogling of this "private" part.

One small school of Freudian scholars reportedly believed the expression, "Crossing that bridge when you get to it" is a reference to the sexual pleasure ancient Man (and Woman) associated with the nose bridge.

One reason that the nose bridge declined as a sexual stimulant in recent times has been blamed on the use of eyeglasses, which have a definite tendency to deaden the nerve endings of this sensuous area.

Stimulation of a senior man's nose bridge is best achieved by rubbing it between your thumb and index finger in a downward motion, which as a side benefit does wonders for relieving any sinus congestion he may have. Such stroking will make even "stuffy" seniors more conducive to further foreplay. Of course, you must be careful not to accidentally poke your partner in an eye as most senior men find this a certain turnoff.

The Adams Apple (Laryngeal Prominence). Generally overlooked because the larynx is so close to other more well-known erogenous areas such as the lips, neck and ears. But, ladies, don't over look this odd-shaped hard mass of machismo. It's there, hidden only from the mind's eye, just challenging you to find it, fondle it, and explore its sensuous secrets. Arousing the Adam's Apple is definitely an external activity and should be done gently. There is nothing romantic about an elderly gentleman gagging.

According to a South Seas elder tribesman who represented his island during the 1970s in the United Nations, elderly women of his tribe have a fetish about the male Adam's Apple. He is quoted as saying (during a tabloid interview) that these women stimulate the A. A. by using their thumbs to pull back on the skin area on both sides of this "forbidden fruit" so that it protrudes noticeably.

They then proceed to excite it orally as if giving it a hickey, but more gently. He noted that as a precaution, senior tribesmen all kept a supply of nitroglycerin pills at their bedsides.

The Posterior Side of Knee Joint. Probably the most erogenous and yet least known senior male arousal area. Before going further, you should first know more about this joyful joint. It contains biceps muscles on top and two leads of the gastrocnemius muscle below. The poples, which is the ham or back surface of the knee, houses the popliteal artery and tibial and common peroneal nerves. This soft plush area when correctly aroused will provide your senior lover moments of ecstasy he never believed possible.

For maximum pleasure, have him lie stomach down on a firm support or mattress. Hold the back of his thigh with one hand and palm his shinbone with the other. Now gently pressing on the thigh, slowly at first and then more quickly bend the knee up and down until you achieve a smooth stroke.

After the knee joint has been properly loosened, you should then also rotate it in a small circle, gradually making the circle larger. (Aside from the erotic benefits of this manipulation, it also beats the hell out of a knee replacement.)

There is historical precedence for extolling the posterior knee joint as an erotic area, particularly in the more frigid zones of the world where such foreplay can be performed while fully clothed, giving it a distinct advantage over many other erogenous areas of the male body.

And now, ladies, you know all there is to understand about a senior male's erogenous zones. Except, of course, for that one in his head, which you will *never* understand.

Some Sample Definitions From the New Senior Sex Dictionary

Times change, and when it does it brings new words into our vocabularies and often brings new meanings to familiar words. So as we grow into our senior years we become acquainted with these new words and with common terms that take on new meanings. All this is especially true in the area of seniors and sex. Following are a few such definitions culled from the latest edition of the Seniors' Sex Dictionary.

ABSTINENCE—The avoidance of goodies and other forbidden foods

BONDAGE—Perverted behavior that has some seniors obsessed with tying up a fixed bond rate of return

CLEAVAGE—What many senior women have more of as a result of sagging breasts

DROPSY—Medical condition in which a senior's upper body weight shifts radically downward

EJACULATION—Noise made when a senior has neglected to take a laxative

ERECTION—An arthritic condition that results in the hardening of any joint

FOREPLAY—a senior's round of golf with three friends

Mike and Jeanne Piedmonte

G-SPOT—Internal device in a credit card machine that gives much pleasure by approving purchases

HEAVY BREATHING—Sound that a senior makes just prior to actual snoring

IMPOTENCE—A serious problem that results from the inability of many senior males to satisfy their spouses in *anything* that they do

JOKE—A brief but accurate description of the sex life of many seniors

KINKY—A severe muscle cramp, often occurring in the calf muscle

LUST—A strong bedroom desire, such as an uninterrupted night's sleep

MENOPAUSE—What senior men do when they see a well-built young woman

MARITAL RELATIONS—When a mother-in-law comes for a long visit

MATINEE—The act of spontaneously going to a movie in the afternoon

NAUGHTY—Description of a senior who habitually takes a second helping of dessert

OLD AGE—Period in a senior's life when neither the spirit nor the flesh is willing or able

PMS—Acronym for Pesty Male Senior

QUICKIE—A sudden need to go to the bathroom

RUNNING AROUND—A senior who has taken up jogging to help with a heart condition

SIZE ANXIETY—An unnecessary preoccupation with dress or trouser sizes

TENDERNESS—The feeling around a muscle ache

URGE—A nicer way to say "nag"

VIRGIN—Type of olive oil best suited for making pasta sauce

WIND—Fiber-induced "colonometer" condition of many seniors

X-RATED—A senior's naked body seen in a full-length mirror and an overhead light

YOUTH—Period of life when nothing sexual is impossible (for antonym, see OLD AGE)

ZIPPER—Name of club many senior heart patients belong to

About The Authors

To help keep his sanity, Mike Piedmonte has been writing humor essays for some 40 years. His articles have appeared in such national publications as Glamour, Mademoiselle, and Christian Science Monitor as well as in numerous other magazines and newspapers. He is the author of a novel entitled, "Split Land of Liberty." After being married to Mike for 46 years Jeanne, to keep her sanity, decided to join Mike in this endeavor. The couple has three children and six grandchildren, all of whom bring them great joy. They enjoy a variety of activities including traveling, cooking, and Tai Chi.